RUTH

A Romance
with Destiny

A Prophetic Look at the Book of Ruth:
Your Divine Destiny—Glory

SALLY SMITH PURVIS

RUTH
A Romance with Destiny
© 2012 Sally Smith Purvis

Unless otherwise noted, all scripture passages are taken from the
King James Version of the Holy Bible.

ISBN: 978-0-9772990-9-6
Published by
Seed of Harvest Ministries
Margate, Florida, United States of America

Printed in Bogota, Colombia

Dear Gayle,

To your glorious destiny in Christ!

Love
Sally

DEDICATION

To my Mother, my spiritual Mom: You have always been a source of encouragement and strength to me throughout my journey.

And, to my Dad who has been an inspiration and the example of a godly man, always demonstrating his love to God first and his family second.

Lastly, but most importantly, this book is dedicated to my Boaz, Jesus Christ. I love You and thank You for loving me and revealing to me Your amazing grace.

ACKNOWLEDGEMENT

The inspiration for this book came from Dr. Kelley Varner. I first met Dr. Varner in 1992 on the way to a conference in West Monroe, Louisiana, when we happened to be on the same flight. At the conference, he preached on the passion of Rizpah who kept vigil "from the beginning of harvest until water dropped from heaven" (2 Samuel 21). I had never encountered a meeting like this: there was spontaneous dance, utterances of the Spirit, declarations, prophetic songs, banners that preached and an electric atmosphere.

This is where I learned of Dr. Varner's correspondence course and his conference in Richlands, North Carolina, and my world changed. I read everything he ever wrote. He profoundly impacted my life and my walk with the Holy Spirit, who is my teacher. I deeply miss Dr. Varner who departed from this realm June 2009, and am honored to provide him this acknowledgement.

FOREWORD

Through the years there have been many thoughts and sermons inspired by the Book of Ruth. There are so many truths and insights in those few chapters that you could spend hours of discovery poring over the nuggets of wisdom found in the story.

As you read this book you will find that Sally has made it so personal that Ruth's journey can become your journey also.

This book is not a feel-good approach to understanding the scripture so you can have success. It is, however, a practical insight into how God always has a plan for those who are faithful.

I have known Sally and her family since she was a young girl, and have watched her mature into an anointed teacher of the Word with a deep understanding of the prophetic nature of the scriptures. Her love relationship with Jesus Christ is real, deep, and unshakeable, and it forms the basis of her character. I am pleased that God used me to prophesy to her that she would write this very book, and also pleased that she is ordained under my ministry.

In RUTH: A ROMANCE WITH DESTINY, Sally Smith Purvis has been able to capture the incredible wisdom and love that our Father God has for His children. It is a book that will encourage your commitment, strengthen your faith and validate your dreams.

— *Bishop Rick Thomas, DD*

TABLE OF CONTENTS

INTRODUCTION

The first message I ever preached, almost twenty years ago, was from the book of Ruth. It was completely spontaneous, certainly not the norm for a girl who grew up in a traditional Presbyterian church. The Holy Spirit just took over, and ever since I have loved this book of divine providence with its wonderful ending of love and desires fulfilled.

Don't we all like a good romance? We celebrate when boy meets girl, they struggle to overcome obstacles to their love, but in the end boy gets girl and they live happily ever after. The happy ending satisfies a basic need in us to believe that love can overcome all odds. Ruth's story contains all the elements of a good romance, but it is much more than that.

Revealing the Hidden

This book delves into the prophetic meaning lying beneath the surface of the story of Ruth. In Mark, after Jesus related the parable of sowing to His disciples, He said, "Is the lamp brought in to be put under a peck measure or under a bed, and not [to be put] on the lampstand? [Things are hidden temporarily only as a means to revelation.] For there is nothing hidden except to be revealed, nor is anything [temporarily] kept secret except in order that it may be made known" (Mark 4:21-22 AMP).

As we follow some basic rules for understanding scripture, the hidden things are revealed by the Holy Spirit. We will examine the original Hebrew to understand the meanings of words, and we will interpret scripture with scripture.

Much of the revelation we will uncover in the book of Ruth is based upon "type and shadow." This means that characters and events in the Old Testament point to and foretell characters and events in the New Testament. One of the most well-known examples is the Passover of the Old Testament. Following the commandment of God as given to Moses, the Israelites smeared the blood of a sacrificial lamb on their doorframes. When the death angel saw the blood, he passed over that household and the Israelites were saved from death. The sacrificial lamb is a "type" of Jesus, the Lamb of God who gave Himself as a sacrifice for our sins. The application of the blood "foreshadows" the shedding of Christ's blood on the cross so that we could be saved.

Similarly, the characters and events in Ruth's story are types and shadows of the New Testament experience that every born-again Christian undergoes as they leave behind the darkness and step into the marvelous light of God's Kingdom.

More than a "Type"

Ruth is more than an Old Testament type. She was a real person, who lived in the time when judges reigned in Israel. Bible historians and commentators believe her story was included in the Bible to provide background for the lineage of King David. However, God does nothing by chance. Ruth was chosen to be included in the lineage of Jesus Christ. Her destiny and purpose are revealed in the story of her remarkable journey.

Ruth's journey is similar to my own. In understanding her journey, I have found my identity and an entry point for the story of my life. I relate to this brave young woman who suffered devastation and overwhelming loss but was willing to leave all that was familiar to her and her native country. She rose above her dysfunctional circumstances, and in her quest for freedom she found love, an incredible destiny and her identity.

What About My Dream, Lord?

Would I be able to rise above my dysfunctional circumstances? Would I find the love of my life and an incredible destiny? My dream as a little girl was to follow in my mother's footsteps—married at eighteen, two children, a loving, Godly husband and a successful career. Yet it seemed that every dream I had ended in failure.

My "Grama" was my closest friend, and she always told me she wanted to live to see my children. She saw me endure two painful divorces and a single, childless life.

When it seemed that marriage and motherhood were eluding me, I focused on a quest for God's truth and finding answers. Most of my spare time was spent seeking God and being in church. I was in church almost every night of the week because I had a need to feel safe and I desired to live a life of purpose. I went to Benny Hinn meetings and traveled across the country pursuing the presence of God. I continually devoured the Word. Then, I was asked to teach a Bible study, which I eventually taught twice a week. As part of a Bible school, I became both student and teacher.

I learned to trust God and trust His timing. I had always desired a mate, and, surely, after five years God would answer my prayer. Certainly after ten. Definitely after fifteen. I kept on fasting and praying and seeking God and devouring the Word. Twenty years—surely now, Lord!

Then I thought God had placed someone in my life. However, I came to see that he was not the one

God had chosen for me. In the same year that I broke off an engagement to that man, the company where I was employed closed its doors, leaving me without an income. It took a year of job-hunting before I finally became employed. At last, some forward momentum! But, five days after starting my new position, I was in an accident that totaled my Mustang convertible and rendered me unable to get out of bed due to excruciating pain. Another roadblock!

You would think all these situations would leave me totally depressed—and they would have were it not for God. At just the right time, God would use someone to speak into my life that He had a plan for me and that the best was yet to come. He sent me hope. So, I persevered even when I did not know what to do. The Word of God led me through every valley. His presence covered me, healed me, and gave me strength to continue my journey.

I love the God that Ruth had learned to trust because it is He Who sustains me, provides for me, protects me, enriches my life with Godly friends and fellowship, and Who shows me again and again that I am His beloved. My story does not end here, but let us journey with Ruth before I tell you what the Author and Finisher of my faith has done.

For it is in Ruth's journey that we will see the unveiling of God's divine providence, not only in this account, but also in our own lives. We will see how God is sovereign and providential as He orchestrates situations to bring about incredible purposes.

We desire to know our purpose because purpose creates value in our lives and creates identity. Understanding our identity ultimately determines our destiny. Ruth found out who she was and *Whose* she was, and it changed everything!

It is my hope that this study will undergird your search for identity and the fulfillment of your destiny.

God knew what he was doing from the very beginning.
He decided from the outset to shape the lives of those
who love Him along the same lines
as the life of His Son . . . .
After God made that decision of what
His children should be like, He followed it up
by calling people by name.

After He called them by name, He set them on a solid
basis with Himself.
And then, after getting them established,
He stayed with them to the end,
gloriously completing what He had begun.
Romans 8:29-30 *The Message*

At the end of each chapter there are questions to help you explore where you are in your own divine romance with the Author and the Finisher of *your* faith. Prepare for greater intimacy with the Lover of your soul, and enjoy the journey!

— *Sally Smith Purvis*

CHAPTER 1

OUT OF MOAB

D o you want everything God has prepared for you? You may think this is a silly question and immediately answer, "Of course I do." I ask that question because most Christians do not live as if we do. We give God an hour or so on Sunday morning and think that is enough. But this is a critical hour in the history of the Church of Jesus Christ. If we Christians do not receive what God has for us, how can we fulfill the purpose and destiny for which we were created? And we cannot receive without developing an intimacy with our Creator.

We of all people need to fellowship with God through the Living Word so we will be a more hopeful, patient and expectant people. This will happen as we experientially become united with the Holy Spirit, our Comforter.

My hunger for the Word and a deeper experience with God did not happen overnight. I have had numerous encounters with famine and failure. I have failed at marriage; my dreams of a family were smashed. A successful college basketball career crumpled with a knee injury. As my hopes were dashed, my Heavenly Father pointed me to eternal Truth, a Person who never disappoints. I have lived in the land of famine, but that is not where my story ends. Likewise, our story of Ruth begins with a famine but that is not where it ends!

> *Now it came to pass in the days when the judges ruled, that there was a famine in the land. And a certain man of Bethlehem Judah went to sojourn in the country of Moab, he, and his wife, and his two sons. And the name of the man was Elimelech, and the name of his wife Naomi, and the name of his two sons Mahlon and Chilion, Ephrathites of Bethlehem Judah. And they came into the country of Moab, and continued there.*
>
> *Ruth 1:1-2 KJV*

What a scene! Elimelech, a Hebrew man whose name means God is King, did not live up to his name. Because there was a famine he chose to move out of Bethlehem Judah. Bethlehem means house of bread and comes from the Hebrew word *"benah"* which means to build or to obtain children. Judah means praise. This family came from a place full of substance and provision (bread), but instead of staying there they went to Moab.

The Meaning of Moab

To understand Moab, we must look first at Sodom, a city so corrupt and perverted that God determined to destroy it. Lot, Abraham's nephew, and his family were allowed to flee the wrath that God rained down upon the city. However, Sodom's spirit of perversion clung to Lot's daughters. They plotted to have their father's child, under the pretext that no men were left in the world, a situation which they knew to be false. (See Genesis 19.) Their ungodly, incestuous relationships—an expression of the carnal nature that brings curses upon succeeding generations, and ultimately, death, produced two sons: Moab and Ben-Ammi. Moab became the father of the Moabites, and his brother, Ben-Ammi, the chief of the Ammonites. The territory given them by God was along the Arnon River, and the people who dwelt there worshipped false gods.

Centuries later, when Moses brought the children of Israel out of Egypt and was taking them to the Promised Land, he sought permission to cross the region of Ar to reach Canaan. Moab and Ammon denied the Israelites access. This angered God who forbade the Israelites from inter-marrying with the Moabites and Ammonites or allowing them to become part of the congregation for a period of ten generations.

However, the Moabites wanted to mingle with the Israelites and instructed their daughters to use their wiles to entice Hebrew men into marriage. The result was not just an intermingling of people groups, but an intermingling of worship of false gods with the worship of the one true God.

Thus, Moab represents places within us where we have tried to mix the Holy Spirit and godliness with ungodliness, double-mindedness, selfishness, compromise, pride, and lack.

The Bible tells us, *"Moab has been at ease from his youth, and he has settled on his lees [like wine] and has not been drawn off from one vessel to another, neither has he gone into exile. Therefore his taste remains in him, and his scent has not changed. Therefore behold, the days are coming, says the Lord, when I shall send to [Moab] tilters who shall tilt him up and shall empty his vessels and break his bottles (earthenware) in pieces"* (Jeremiah 48:11-12 AMP).

Moab was idle and allowed compromise and did not want to change or grow. He did not allow a fresh move of God. In other words, Moab was like a stagnant pond, covered with reeking algae. Rather than change, he preferred self-centeredness.

There was a time in my life when I dwelt in Moab. I was stuck in a religious mindset and had a sense of lack; I limited God. My thinking was that God was a hard taskmaster, and even though I grew up in the Church, I did not feel like I measured up to His love and standards. Deep down, I accused God of treating me inadequately, feeling that I ended up with the short end of the stick. This is a Moab mindset that misjudges Almighty God.

The prophet Isaiah speaks of Moab's pride, *"We have heard of the pride of Moab, that he is very proud — even* of his arrogance, his conceit, his wrath, his untruthful boasting" (Isaiah 16:6 AMP).

Pride and independence kept me from admitting how hurt and offended I was. I wanted to appear strong and unaffected. Pride delayed my dealing with truth and so I stayed in a place of unforgiveness.

In your own life, have you changed in the last year? Do you trust God more? Are you moving forward and forgetting the past? Have you forgiven everyone for everything? Are you expecting the supernatural? The Word says to be changed from faith to faith, from strength to strength, and from glory to glory.

Sin's Wages: Death

And Elimelech Naomi's husband died; and she was left, and her two sons. And they took them wives of the women of Moab; the name of the one was Orpah, and the name of the other Ruth: and they dwelled there about ten years. And Mahlon and Chilion died also both of them; and the woman was left of her two sons and her husband.
Ruth 1:3-5

The consequences of dwelling in Moab, in sin, are painful. Ten years is a long time to be away from the place of praise and the house of bread. Verse 1 says they "went to sojourn," meaning it was their intent to stay only temporarily in Moab. However, verse 2 says they "continued there." They became entangled in Moabite business and delayed their departure. Finally, verse 4 says, "they dwelled there about ten years."

We need to be careful of the ties or associations we make. These relationships are not just with physical people, places and things; these can be interactions in our own mind or emotions. When we rehearse a negative situation or nurse bitterness or regret, we end up forgetting the house of bread and the house of praise, and we forfeit God's best.

Both sons, Mahlon and Chilion, died in Moab. Mahlon's name means sick or sickly, and the name Chilion means weakening or pining. Elimelech and Naomi took their sons to a place birthed out of carnality, and the result was death. Paul tells us, "For the wages of sin is death" (Romans 6:23), and "to be carnally minded is death" (Romans 8:6).

In other words, the decisions we make without divine guidance always lead to disappointment and lack of fulfillment.

Naomi, Ruth, and Orpah now find themselves in a desperate situation. They have much to grieve about. Not only have they suffered great loss, but also they have been away from the house of praise and bread far too long.

We have all experienced loss, pain, separation, and extreme disappointment— all the more reason to stay on the journey. God is no respecter of persons. What God did for Ruth and Naomi, He wants to do for you. We will see the providence and faithfulness of God truly working all things together for our good.

Hope in the House!

Then she arose with her daughters in law,
that she might return from the country of Moab: for
she had heard in the country of Moab
how that the LORD had visited his people
in giving them bread.
Ruth 1:6

It took a lot of courage and strength for Naomi to get up out of her familiar place of discouragement, depression and despair—to arise. But her circumstances made her so uncomfortable, she had to leave. No matter where you are, in whatever area of Moab you find yourself, whatever place of mixture, compromise or sin, God is able to send His Spirit to speak and cause His voice to be heard. Even in the midst of depression and oppression, God can cause you to remember that there is fresh bread in His house. You cannot flee from the presence of God; He is always speaking and inviting us to a higher place out of limitation and lack.

The psalmist David writes.

> *Where could I go from Your Spirit?*
> *Or where could I flee from Your presence?*
> *If I ascend up into heaven, You are there;*
> *if I make my bed in Sheol (the place of the dead),*
> *behold, You are there.*
> *If I take the wings of the morning or dwell in the uttermost parts of the sea, even there shall Your hand lead me, and Your right hand shall hold me.*
> *If I say, Surely the darkness shall cover me and the night shall be [the only] light about me, even*

the darkness hides nothing from You,
but the night shines as the day; the darkness and the
light are both alike to You.
Psalms 139:7-12 AMP

There is nothing like the visitation of the Lord! The presence of God is light and in it we are able to see His provision, purpose and our destiny. As you open your heart to Him, His words to you become spirit and life. Just like Naomi heard the message that the Lord had visited His people and given them bread, just so, the Holy Spirit wants to nourish and impart hope to you right now.

Jesus then said to them, I assure you, most solemnly I
tell you, Moses did not give you the Bread from heaven
[what Moses gave you was not the Bread from heav-
en], but it is My Father Who gives you the true heav-
enly Bread. For the Bread of God is He Who comes
down out of heaven and gives life to the world. Then
they said to Him, Lord, give us this bread always (all
the time)! Jesus replied, I am the Bread of Life. He who
comes to Me will never be hungry, and he who believes
in and cleaves to and trusts in and relies on Me will
never thirst any more (at any time).
John 6:32-35 AMP

He is the remedy, the cure, and the answer; but, we have to choose to come to Him. This bread is living, full of life. What are you eating? Jesus is the bread, but you have to consume it to make it a part of you. The saying really is true, "You are what you eat."

Faith Hears and Responds

Wherefore she went forth out of the place where she was, and her two daughters in law with her; and they went on the way to return unto the land of Judah.

Ruth 1:7

Imagine the excitement and trepidation on this great day of leaving the old and returning to the land of praise. There is much prophetic significance for us today if we lay hold of this! As we leave Moab and return to praise, the mighty Lion of the tribe of Judah inhabits that praise, and the door to an adventurous life worth living swings wide.

You see, the place the women were leaving was full of disappointments, unbelief, and regret; but, in the atmosphere of praise those enemies must depart. The word says, "But thou art holy, O Thou that inhabitest the praises of Israel" (Psalm 22:3 KJV). They were about to cross out of a place where they had been held captive, and move into a land of sustenance and freedom.

Similarly, the father of our faith, Abraham, was called to leave his land of birth. The Lord told Abram: "Get out of your country, from your family and from your father's house, to a land that I will show you" (Genesis 12:1 NKJV).

Imagine God coming to you and saying, "I know you have lived in this town your whole life, and all of your family is here; but I want you to pack up and leave it all behind. Leave everything that is familiar to you. I will not show you where you are going until you are on the road. You have to trust Me that I have something better for you." How frightening to leave both what and who you have known for so long to set out into the unknown! But Abraham was obedient; he had eyes of faith.

"For he was [waiting expectantly and confidently] looking forward to the city which has fixed and firm foundations, whose Architect and Builder is

God" (Hebrews 11:10 AMP). Abraham went through seven separations or critical choices of obedience to God which, in turn, brought about a fresh revelation from God and produced a new level of worship in Abraham. Three of them are presented here. Similarly, in our own lives, God presents us with critical choices of obedience to reveal persons, places and things that we need to disconnect from in order to fulfill destiny and purpose.

Faith's Complete Consecration

Now the Lord had said to Abraham:
Get out of your country, from your family and from
your father's house, to a land that I will show you.
Genesis 12:1 NKJV

Abraham's first separation occurred when he left the country of Ur. A country is a region or a land within a boundary or border. Perhaps it is the place where our identity is bound up. The land within our boundary can be a place of natural ties that are more important to us than God. For me it was a denominational church system that God called me to leave.

30

God is a jealous God who loves us and wants our very best.

The second separation Abraham faced was from kindred or close ties. Genesis 12:4-5 says, "So Abram departed as the LORD had spoken to him, and Lot went with him. And Abram was seventy-five years old when he departed from Haran. Then Abram took Sarai his wife and Lot his brother's son, and all their possessions that they had gathered, and the people whom they had acquired in Haran, and they departed to go to the land of Canaan." (NKJV)

Abraham did not completely obey God's command to leave his father's house and his family. Since he had no child of his own, it was natural for him to take his nephew Lot, the son of Abraham's brother Haran, who had died. There was security and comfort in having someone from home along on the journey into the unknown.

However, the relationship between Abraham and Lot grew strained as they each had great possessions, herds and herdsmen. Quarreling broke out between their herdsmen over the use of the land, and finally, Abraham separated from Lot. Abraham allowed Lot to choose the territory he wanted for himself, and Lot chose as his own the plain of Jordan.

Lot's name means a covering or veil. The flesh is a type of a veil that covers the glory of God. We likewise must separate from security blankets so we can experience the fullness that God intends. Is there something or someone you need to release so you can move forward in the things of God?

The final separation Abraham had to endure was from Isaac, the promised son. In Genesis 22, "...*God tested and proved Abraham and said to him, Abraham! And he said, Here I am. [God] said, Take now your son, your only son Isaac, whom you love, and go to the region of Moriah; and offer him there as a burnt offering upon one of the mountains of which I will tell you* (vv 1-2 AMP).

Abraham had already had to separate from his son, Ishmael, and now God was calling him to sacrifice his delight and heir. Imagine the heavy heart with which Abraham made the journey to Mount Moriah, and lashed his beloved son to the altar. Yet, even then, he was obedient to God.

Sometimes we have to ask ourselves if we love the promise of God more than the God of the promise. The lesson of the faith walk of Abraham is that nothing compares to the glory and presence of God. "But as it is written, Eye hath not seen, nor ear heard, neither have entered into the heart of man, the things which God hath prepared for them that love him" (1 Corinthians 2:9). As the Spirit imparts to us His truth, we are empowered to leave what limits or entangles us and move by faith into new territories.

Returning to God

There are key words in scripture that express the same thought. *Return* is one such word pregnant with meaning. It conveys the idea of to restore, recover, repair, refresh or revive. Let's explore some "returns" in scripture because this is what God is doing in our lives.

"And the ransomed of the LORD shall return, and come to Zion with songs and everlasting joy upon their heads: they shall obtain joy and gladness, and sorrow and sighing shall flee away" (Isaiah 35:10).

"Come, and let us return to the Lord; for He has torn, but He will heal us; He has stricken, but He will bind us up. After two days He will revive us; on the third day He will raise us up, that we may live in His sight" (Hosea 6:1-2 NKJV).

Returning to the land of praise is where we embrace and enforce the victory. As we return to the Lord in this day, He will raise us up so we live and move and have our being in Him. In His presence, in His glory, there is a change on the inside. Like David says,

> *You will show me the path of life,*
> *in Your presence is fullness of joy,*
> *at Your right hand there are pleasures forevermore.*
> Psalm 16:11 AMP

As we make a conscious decision to return to Him, sorrow, depression, and mourning will flee.

The returning of Naomi and Ruth models what we are called to do today: "So repent (change your mind and purpose); turn around and return [to God], that your sins may be erased (blotted out, wiped clean), that times of refreshing (of recovering from the effects of heat, of reviving with fresh air) may come from the presence of the Lord..." (Acts 3:19 AMP).

We are called to turn from the place of our sinfulness, our Moab, and return to Him, the Shepherd of our soul, just as Peter declares, "For ye were as sheep going astray; but are now returned unto the Shepherd and Bishop of your souls" (1 Peter 2:25). Our Shepherd is leading us beside still waters to restore our minds, wills and emotions.

Will You Follow?

And Naomi said unto her two daughters in law, Go, return each to her mother's house: the LORD deal kindly with you, as ye have dealt with the dead, and with me. The LORD grant you that ye may find rest, each of you in the house of her husband. Then she kissed them; and they lifted up their voice, and wept. And they said unto her, Surely we will return with thee unto thy people. And Naomi said, Turn again, my daughters: why will ye go with me? are there yet any more sons in my womb, that they may be your husbands? Turn again, my daughters, go your way; for I am too old to have an husband. If I should say, I

have hope, if I should have an husband also tonight,
and should also bear sons; Would ye tarry for them till
they were grown? would ye stay for them from having
husbands? nay, my daughters; for it grieveth me much
for your sakes that the hand of the LORD is gone out
against me. And they lifted up their voice, and wept
again: and Orpah kissed her mother in law; but Ruth
clave unto her. And she said, Behold, thy sister in law
is gone back unto her people, and unto her gods: return
thou after thy sister in law.
Ruth 1:8-15

Naomi prayed for Ruth and Orpah, and held a pity party riddled with doubts and questions. Then she accused God for the situation for which she herself is responsible. God does not show up in our pity parties, but He is moved by faith. Orpah turned back, but Ruth made a wise decision, which has affected all of human history. Her resolution released divine destiny into her life.

Ruth's Conversion and Baptism

And Ruth said, Intreat me not to leave thee, or to re-
turn from following after thee: for whither thou goest, I

will go; and where thou lodgest, I will lodge: thy peo-
ple shall be my people, and thy God my God: Where
thou diest, will I die, and there will I be buried: the
LORD do so to me, and more also, if ought but death
part thee and me. When she saw that she was stead-
fastly minded to go with her, then she left speaking un-
to her.
Ruth 1:16-18

Yes, Ruth was determined. Through her years in living with her husband and Naomi, Ruth must have seen a testimony of the Living God in Naomi. How the holiness of the family's worship of the One True God must have contrasted with the unholy worship of the Moabite gods!

In the valley of her decision, Ruth chose to follow Naomi and her God. This is an Old Testament "type" of the decision we make for salvation, and for Ruth, it is her initial salvation experience. Do you need to say "yes" to following God or surrendering more completely?

Not only does Ruth make a salvation decision—choosing the God of holiness—but she also speaks words that foreshadow the ritual of baptism:

"Where thou diest, will I die, and there will I be buried." In the New Testament the Apostle Paul explains, "Know ye not, that so many of us as were baptized into Jesus Christ were baptized into His death? Therefore we are buried with Him by baptism into death: that like as Christ was raised up from the dead by the glory of the Father, even so we also should walk in newness of life" (Romans 6:3-4).

Ruth is progressing into her future, moving forward by forsaking her past. She was willing to leave all that she knew for a very uncertain future. I am sure that on the dusty journey toward Bethlehem there must have been many challenges, but she was steadfast and committed.

Just like Ruth who showed a determination for a fresh start, we, too, can have a mind that is in harmony with the heavens. Paul gave us a clue by saying, "I beseech you therefore, brethren, by the mercies of God, that you present your bodies a living sacrifice, holy, acceptable to God, which is your reasonable service. And do not be conformed to this world, but be transformed by the renewing of your mind, that you may prove what is that good and acceptable and perfect will of God" (Romans 12:1-2).

Naomi and Ruth Move a City

So they two went until they came to Bethlehem
and it came to pass, when they were come to Bethlehem,
that all the city was moved about them, and
they said, Is this Naomi?
Ruth 1:19

Imagine the talk: Naomi, the Jew, returns to Bethlehem after many years, and she has with her a Moabitess, Ruth, who is now Abraham's seed! Naomi, however, is not a happy woman.

Naomi Blames God

And she said unto them, Call me not Naomi,
call me Mara: for the Almighty hath dealt very bitter-
ly with me. I went out full, and the Lord hath brought
me home again empty: why then call ye me Naomi,
seeing the Lord hath testified against me, and
the Almighty hath afflicted me?
Ruth 1:20-21

The name Naomi means pleasant, but Naomi no longer saw herself as pleasant. She renamed herself, blaming God for her husband's mistake. God never told them to leave Bethlehem for Moab. However, from her clouded perspective Naomi had decided that all the devastation in her life was God's fault. In her resentment and bitterness she labeled herself accordingly, but incorrectly.

How many times in our disappointment and bitterness do we place blame and misjudge God for our wrong decisions? The truth is that He is our provider, sustainer, and all-powerful redeemer Who loves us. Thank God, He gives us new beginnings and a fresh start for each day. Be encouraged as you read this passage.

"But this I recall and therefore have I hope and expectation: It is because of the Lord's mercy and loving-kindness that we are not consumed, because His [tender] compassions fail not." (*See also Malachi 3:6.*) "They are new every morning; great and abundant is Your stability and faithfulness" (Lamentations 3:21-23 AMP). (*See also Isaiah 33:2.*)

Paul explains, "For as many of you as have been baptized into Christ have put on Christ. There is neither Jew nor Greek, there is neither bond nor free, there is neither male nor female: for ye are all one in Christ Jesus. And if ye be Christ's, then are ye Abraham's seed, and heirs according to the promise" (Gal 3:27-29).

When we understand we are heirs, we will never question our value or worth again. We need to live according to our rights and privileges and search out what the promises are.

Barley Harvest

So Naomi returned, and Ruth the Moabitess, her daughter in law, with her, which returned out of the country of Moab: and they came to Bethlehem in the beginning of barley harvest.

Ruth 1:22

This is one of those examples where God uses people, places and things to bring about His will. When we are submitted to Him, He leads us to the right place with the right people at just the right time. Naomi returned to Bethlehem at the beginning of barley harvest with a "seed" for an unprecedented harvest. Ruth is God's remedy to resolve the affliction and bitterness Naomi has endured. There is a miracle in the making! As we will see, Ruth ends up marrying Boaz, a wealthy landowner, and they have a son who is in the lineage of the Messiah.

So many times in our lives we are so close to fullness and to the manifestation of the supernatural answer, but we are simply unaware. We blame God for our state of affairs when in actuality our situation is full of potential and promise. We cannot see beyond our disappointments and failures.

That is why we need to pray that God would open the eyes of our heart to have the right perspective. "We do not look at the things which are seen, but at the things which are not seen. For the things which are seen are temporary, but the things which are not seen are eternal" (2 Corinthians 4:18 NKJV).

There is more to you than what you see because you have the resurrected life of Christ within. God has prepared things for us that can only be seen by the Spirit. "Now we have received, not the spirit of the world, but the Spirit who is from God, that we might know the things that have been freely given to us by God" (1 Corinthians 2:12 NKJV).

Let us return to Bethlehem, the house of bread; let us return to the place of praise and rejoicing. Naomi and Ruth returned at just the right time. Even when promises seem to be delayed, God has a set time for the unfolding of His plan. His word says, "He has made everything beautiful in its time" (Ecclesiastes 3:11).

Barley was the first of the grains to ripen, about the time of Passover. It is a first fruits harvest and a type of the feast of Passover representing our initial salvation experience. "Speak unto the children of Israel and say unto them, When ye be come into the land I give unto you, and shall reap the harvest thereof, then ye shall bring a sheaf of the firstfruits of your harvest unto the priest" (Leviticus 23:10). "For even Christ our passover is sacrificed for us…" (1 Corinthians 5:7). Jesus our redeemer has paid the price for our sins. The Apostle Paul says, "But now is Christ risen from the dead, and become the firstfruits of them that slept. For since by man came death, by man came also the resurrection of the dead. For as in Adam all die, even so in Christ shall

all be made alive" (1 Corinthians 15:20-22). That is good news! In Christ we shall all be made alive.

Before we continue, we need a fresh repentance or a changing of our mind. Every experience with God requires a setting apart of our lives unto Him and a decision to leave Moab for the realm of life in His presence. Revelation 21:5 says, "Then He who sat on the throne said, 'Behold, I make all things new.' And He said to me, 'Write, for these words are true and faithful.'" (NKJV)

Personal Application

- Like Ruth, what changes do you feel the Holy Spirit is asking you to make?

- Did the Holy Spirit reveal any areas of "Moab" in your life? If so, what are they?

- It is time to live in "Bethlehem Judah." What does that mean to you?

Chapter 2

GOD GUIDES

I n Chapter One, Ruth made significant progress. She left Moab and turned her back on everything she had known and with her words and actions pledged allegiance to Naomi and Naomi's God. She demonstrated a willingness to change. God desires to remove from us every obstacle that hinders and to draw us completely to Himself. In His presence we can experience a divine romance.

Truth Guides

Just as Naomi and Ruth were guided to Bethlehem at the right season, God is able to safely lead you to your destination. John 16:13 tells us, "Howbeit when He, the Spirit of truth, is come, He will guide you into all truth: for He shall not speak of Himself; but whatsoever He shall hear, that shall He speak: and He will shew you things to come."

Scripture says, "The king's heart is in the hand of the LORD, as the rivers of water: He turneth it whithersoever He will" (Proverbs 21:1). Recently I had a dream in which I was in a canoe going down a river. Of its own accord, the canoe veered 180 degrees to go through a tunnel that I did not even see at first. I felt this was the Lord saying, "I am in control of your direction, trust Me." We have a sovereign God. When we are submitted to Him, we make plans, but He orders our steps.

Kinsman Boaz

*And Naomi had a kinsman of her husband's, a mighty
man of wealth, of the family of Elimelech;
and his name was Boaz.*

Ruth 2:1

The name *"Boaz"* in Hebrew means fleetness.
The dictionary defines fleetness as the ability to be
swift or rapid. Boaz is also the name given to one of
the two brazen pillars erected in the porch of Solomon's temple. In our story, Boaz is a "type" of the
Lord Jesus Christ, the ultimate Kinsman-redeemer.

The law of the kinsman-redeemer is found in Leviticus 25:48-49. A poor person who fell upon difficult circumstances could be redeemed from debt by
a family member or blood relative.

Jesus is our Kinsman-redeemer or elder brother.
The Apostle Paul explains, "He who did not spare
his own Son, but gave Him up for us all—how will
He not also, along with Him, graciously give us all
things?" (Romans 8:32 NIV).

When we are redeemed, we are made part of the
family of God through the work of Jesus Christ.

"God, for whom and through whom everything was made, chose to bring many children into glory. And it was only right that He should make Jesus, through His suffering, a perfect leader, fit to bring them into their salvation. So now Jesus and the ones He makes holy have the same Father. That is why Jesus is not ashamed to call them His brothers and sisters" (Hebrews 2:10-11 NLT).

On the Mercy Seat in the Most Holy Place in the Tabernacle of Moses are two cherubim. The cherubim were constructed of one piece of gold, representing that we come from one source. God gave Moses these specific instructions for the cherubim: "And thou shalt make a mercy seat of pure gold: two cubits and a half shall be the length thereof, and a cubit and a half the breadth thereof. And thou shalt make two cherubims of gold, of beaten work shalt thou make them, in the two ends of the mercy seat. And make one cherub on the one end, and the other cherub on the other end: even of the mercy seat shall ye make the cherubims on the two ends thereof" (Exodus 25:17-19 KJV).

Jesus is our Kinsman, and we are joined to Him through the act of salvation and made one with the Lord.

Boaz is a Mighty Man of Wealth

The earthly Boaz, who represents Christ, our Redeemer, was a man of substance, with lands, servants, and resources.

The word "mighty" in Hebrew means strong, valiant, upright, champion or chief, to prevail, and to confirm a covenant. Daniel, the Old Testament prophet and dream interpreter, prophesied that our redeemer would come to confirm the covenant and promise of the New Covenant. Christ, our Redeemer, has come to confirm that which was written and fully paid for by His blood.

"And He shall confirm the covenant with many for one week: and in the midst of the week He shall cause the sacrifice and the oblation to cease..." (Daniel 9:27 KJV). Jesus is a covenant keeper and is committed to you. Our Kinsman is mighty, worthy of our trust and utmost confidence.

Not only is He mighty, He is also wealthy. "Wealth" comes from a Hebrew word, *chayil*, meaning: army, man of valor, valiant, power, ability, riches, substance; and from *chuwl* meaning: pained, travail, dance, calve, to bring forth. Jesus, our mighty, wealthy One, has the ability to bring forth His nature and character within us.

What causes His nature to be birthed within us is His voice. David declares, "The voice of the LORD maketh the hinds to calve, and discovereth the forests: and in His temple doth every one speak of his glory" (Psalm 29:9 KJV). His voice or sound causes and produces new life.

The Word tells us, "The Lord your God is in the midst of you, a Mighty One, a Savior [Who saves]! He will rejoice over you with joy; He will rest [in silent satisfaction] and in His love He will be silent and make no mention [of past sins, or even recall them]; He will exult over you with singing" (Zephaniah 3:17 AMP).

Our heavenly Boaz is not only wealthy; He is by nature a giver and our provider. Paul says, "And my God will liberally supply (fill to the full) your every need according to His riches in glory in Christ Jesus" (Philippians 4:19 AMP).

Ruth's Faith Confession

And Ruth the Moabitess said unto Naomi, Let me now go to the field, and glean ears of corn after him in whose sight I shall find grace. And she said unto her, Go, my daughter.
Ruth 2:2

Ruth had a positive outlook on the future and her confession, "I shall find grace", is admirable.

I wonder if she read this passage from Job: "Thou shalt also decree a thing, and it shall be established unto thee: and the light shall shine upon thy ways" (Job 22:28). David penned a similar thought, "Whoever offers praise glorifies Me; And to him who orders his conduct aright, I will show the salvation of God" (Psalm 50:23 NKJV).

We see in Ruth a willing, submissive and humble heart, and that is the type of person to whom God gives favor. The words we declare are seeds that will produce a harvest. Let's determine to agree with

God and speak in a language of victory that creates life.

Happenstance? Hardly!

And she went, and came, and gleaned in the field after the reapers: and her hap was to light on a part of the field belonging unto Boaz, who was of the kindred of Elimelech.
Ruth 2:3

Light was shining on Ruth's way. She ordered her conversation and God ordered her steps. Ruth was in the midst of a miracle in the making even though she was gleaning in the corners of the field as the Law of Moses provided.

"And when ye reap the harvest of your land, thou shalt not make clean riddance of the corners of thy field when thou reapest, neither shalt thou gather any gleaning of thy harvest: thou shalt leave them unto the poor, and to the stranger:

I am the LORD your God."
Leviticus 23:22

Ruth was poor, hungry, and a stranger in the corner of the field, but this was all part of the process. Similarly in my own life, there was a time when I was hungry and desperate for truth and answers so I spent much time in the Word gleaning for answers—really for my own survival.

A relationship in which I was often a target of sudden verbal and physical abuse had left my heart in need of healing and hope. Lord, how could this happen to me!?! How could I have been so blind? If I could be so wrong about someone, how could I ever trust again? I needed answers, and in those days of questioning and turmoil the only place to find those answers and comfort was in the Living Word. I knew God had a plan and purpose for my life, even though the path was quite unclear to me. With time and deep study of the Word, I found the answers that healed my broken heart, a living and loving relationship with the Truth that sustained me and restored me to wholeness.

Little did I know then that it would be twenty years before God would unite me with the man of my dreams. And little did I know that God would use me to share with the nations the Word I spent years feeding upon.

Even more amazing to consider is that the birth of Jesus in Bethlehem generations later would be dependent on Ruth going to glean ears of corn in the right field.

"Corn" — more accurately wheat, is the most important cereal plant producing edible seeds mentioned in the Bible. More importantly it represents the Word of God, which is a seed. In the gospel of Mark, the kingdom is referred to in the context of grain.

And He said, So is the kingdom of God, as if a man should cast seed into the ground; And should sleep, and rise night and day, and the seed should spring and grow up, he knoweth not how. For the earth bringeth forth fruit of herself; first the blade, then the ear, after that the full corn in the ear.
Mark 4:26-28 KJV

Another reference to corn is found in the book of Joshua. "And they did eat of the old corn of the land on the morrow after the passover, unleavened cakes, and parched corn in the selfsame day. And the manna ceased on the morrow after they had eaten of the old corn of the land; neither had the children of Israel manna any more; but they did eat of the fruit of the land of Canaan that year" (Joshua 5:11-12).

There was a new season for the Israelites so they had a change of diet.

Grain was the fruit of the Promised Land, but the deeper application is that it points us to Jesus who is the kernel of wheat that had to die to produce a harvest. "Verily, verily, I say unto you, Except a corn of wheat fall into the ground and die, it abideth alone: but if it die, it bringeth forth much fruit" (John 12:24). Just as the fruit of Ruth's labors were not seen immediately, neither is the fullness of the fruit of the death of Jesus visible yet, but harvest

time is coming! The Word is true, "Be not deceived;
God is not mocked: for whatsoever a man soweth,
that shall he also reap" (Galatians 6:7).

Ruth had a "hap", a quaint old word for fate or
chance. God orchestrates many "haps" in our lives if
we open our eyes and are aware to see His divine
sovereign providence. In Hebrew, the word trans-
lated as "hap" means befall, event, happening, for-
tune, accident, chance, fate, to meet without prear-
rangement, to build with beams. Perhaps you are in
a "hap" right now and this book may be the provision to catapult you to your next level in God. Many
people could testify of divine, happy accidents that
only God could arrange. God allows various encounters in our lives for the purpose of building the
nature and character of Christ in us so that His purpose is manifested.

God arranged sovereign set-ups that have
changed the course of my destiny by divine inter-
vention on many occasions. One "hap" is the writ-
ing of this book. I had just received some very dev-
astating news that had shaken apart what I thought
would be my future. I was confused and desperately
seeking God's direction. It so *happened* that a long-

time pastor friend was hosting a conference and the speaker that night was my pastor, Bishop Rick Thomas. The Holy Spirit fell and he called me out and prophesied to me about this very book.

An Ordered and Unified Field

And behold, Boaz came from Bethlehem, and said unto the reapers, The LORD be with you. And they answered him, The LORD bless thee. Then said Boaz unto his servant that was set over the reapers, Whose damsel is this?
Ruth 2:4-5

The reapers in the field harvested the crop as a result of effort and labor. The reaper is similar to those with a heart for winning the lost. The servant would be a type of the five-fold ministry gift who has the responsibility to see that the harvest comes to maturity.

The apostle Paul explains the ministry gifts and their function: "And he gave some, apostles; and some, prophets; and some, evangelists; and some, pastors and teachers; for the perfecting of the saints, for the work of the ministry, for the edifying of the body of Christ: Till we all come in the unity of the faith, and of the knowledge of the Son of God, unto a perfect man, unto the measure of the stature of the fulness of Christ" (Ephesians 4:11-13).

The First Encounter

And the servant that was set over the reapers answered
and said, It is the Moabitish damsel that came back
with Naomi out of the country of Moab: And she
said, I pray you, let me glean and gather after the
reapers among the sheaves: so she came, and hath con-
tinued even from the morning until now, that she tar-
ried a little in the house. Then said Boaz unto Ruth,
Hearest thou not, my daughter?
Go not to glean in another field, neither go from hence,
but abide here fast by my maidens:
Ruth 2:6-8

Ruth progressed pretty quickly! Boaz noticed her and their introduction began. She seemed to have learned the power of answered prayer. She had asked to glean and gather after the reapers, but Boaz extended grace and instructed her to stay near the maidens.

The first word Boaz said to her was "hearest". This emphasis on hearing is seen in the Gospels and was taught by Jesus: "Therefore take heed how you hear. For whoever has, to him more will be given; and whoever does not have, even what he seems to have will be taken from him" (Luke 8:18). "Hearing" must be very important, since that is the first thing Boaz says to Ruth.

The voices we listen to will either produce faith or fear. Are we listening to words of life and truth or unbelief, doubt and lies? Adam demonstrated the consequences of listening to the wrong voice. "And the LORD God called unto Adam, and said unto Him, Where art thou? And he said, I heard thy voice in the garden, and I was afraid, because I was naked; and I hid myself. And He said, Who told thee that thou wast naked? Hast thou eaten of the tree, whereof I commanded thee that thou should-est not eat?" (Genesis 3:9-11).

Adam listened to the voice of the enemy who comes to steal, kill and destroy. The voice Adam listened to deceived him and wreaked havoc on the entire human race. But God's word brings life and peace. The more we hear and understand the voice of God through being in close relationship with Him, the more clear and bright is our path in the field God has designed for us.

God desires for us to be fruitful and multiply, and Boaz made certain that Ruth's efforts would be productive.

This Encounter Produces Worship

Let thine eyes be on the field that they do reap,
and go thou after them: have I not charged the young
men that they shall not touch thee?
and when thou art athirst, go unto the vessels, and
drink of that which the young men have drawn.
Then she fell on her face, and bowed herself to the
ground, and said unto him, Why have I found grace
in thine eyes, that thou shouldest take knowledge of me,
seeing I am a stranger?
Ruth 2:9-10

Boaz demonstrated a marvelous example of grace and took special care of Ruth. She was a foreigner, as we all are, "But God commendeth His love toward us, in that, while we were yet sinners, Christ died for us" (Romans 5:8). The more we understand the love of God and His abundant provision for us, the more our response will be to worship.

God Sees All

And Boaz answered and said unto her,
It hath fully been shewed me, all that thou hast done
unto thy mother in law since the death
of thine husband:
and how thou hast left thy father and thy mother, and
the land of thy nativity, and art come unto a people
which thou knewest not heretofore.
Ruth 2:11

Just as it was revealed to Boaz all the sacrifices Ruth made in her journey, nothing goes unnoticed by our heavenly Boaz. Boaz understood the faith it took for Ruth to make the long trip from Moab to Bethlehem, not knowing her fate because the Jews were not to have dealings with Moabites. Boaz mentioned how she treated Naomi since the death of her husband, Mahlon. Mahlon means sickly or weak and can represent a type of the law, that is, the old unspiritual self that we need to reckon dead. Paul explained in the book of Romans:

> *"Know ye not, brethren, (for I speak to them that know the law,) how that the law hath dominion over a man as long as he liveth? For the woman which hath an husband is bound by the law to her husband so long as he liveth; but if the husband be dead, she is loosed from the law of her husband. So then if, while her husband liveth, she be married to another man, she shall be called an adulteress: but if her husband be dead, she is free from that law; so that she is no adulteress, though she be married to another man. Wherefore, my brethren, ye also are become dead to the law by the body of Christ; that ye should be married to another, even to him who is raised from the dead, that we should bring forth fruit unto God"* (Romans 7:1-4).

In other words, we need to understand that the old man—the first husband (the law of sin and death) has been crucified. "Knowing this, that our old man is crucified with him, that the body of sin might be destroyed, that henceforth we should not serve sin" (Romans 6:6). Here is the reason: so that we can be completely joined and married to Christ Jesus and to bring forth good fruit.

The Lord is the Source

*The LORD recompense thy work, and a full reward
be given thee of the LORD God of Israel,
under whose wings thou art come to trust.*
Ruth 2:12

When we look to the Lord, we will not be disappointed. Ruth, in committing her future to Naomi and to the God Naomi served, showed faith. Hebrews 11:6 says, "But without faith it is impossible to please Him, for he who comes to God must believe that He is, and that He is a rewarder of those who diligently seek Him." (NKJV)

Moses had respect for God's reward, too: "By faith Moses, when he became of age, refused to be called the son of Pharaoh's daughter, choosing rather to suffer affliction with the people of God than to enjoy the passing pleasures of sin, esteeming the reproach of Christ greater riches than the treasures in Egypt; for he looked to the reward" (Hebrews 11:24-26).

Look at what God said to Abraham, "... the word of the LORD came unto Abram in a vision, saying, Fear not, Abram: I am thy shield, and thy exceeding great reward" (Genesis 15:1).

Ruth had found the secret place of trust under the wings of the Lord God of Israel. David declares, "He that dwelleth in the secret place of the most High shall abide under the shadow of the Almighty. I will say of the LORD, He is my refuge and my fortress: my God; in Him will I trust. Surely He shall deliver thee from the snare of the fowler, and from the noisome pestilence. He shall cover thee with His feathers, and under His wings shalt thou trust: His truth shall be thy shield and buckler" (Psalm 91:1-4). Amen!

I Want Favor

Then she said, Let me find favour in thy sight,
my lord; for that thou hast comforted me, and
for that thou hast spoken friendly unto thine hand-
maid, though I be not like unto
one of thine handmaidens.
Ruth 2:13

Obviously Ruth wanted favor with Boaz. When Ruth first came to the field she was looking for food because she was hungry, but then she looked directly to Boaz for favor. I read a great definition of favor by Bishop Joseph Garlington:

> *Favor is the unseen but unrelenting, irresistible and supernaturally powerful synergy of the Holy Spirit, preceding, interceding and succeeding on behalf of those in whom God has a loving interest, purpose and plan, in order to create an atmosphere—in any environment-in all of His creation, that must yield absolute and complete compliance to His will, that will ultimately bring glory to His name, if and when a timely and persistent demand is placed upon it.*

Ruth put a demand on "favor," and as we will see, it ultimately brought glory to His name. Ruth demonstrated a grateful heart for all Boaz had done.

She acknowledged how he comforted her. In our own lives the Holy Spirit is a constant companion. Jesus declared: "And I will pray the Father, and He shall give you another Comforter, that He may abide with you for ever; even the Spirit of truth; whom the world cannot receive, because it seeth Him not, neither knoweth Him: but ye know Him; for He dwelleth with you, and shall be in you" (John 14:16-17).

Prayer Granted

And Boaz said unto her, At mealtime come thou hither, and eat of the bread, and dip thy morsel in the vinegar. And she sat beside the reapers: and he reached her parched corn, and she did eat, and was sufficed, and left.
Ruth 2:14

I'd like to know how Ruth's prayer was answered so soon! She had a date with destiny at mealtime. Boaz invited her to eat with him and, notice, he fed her. Our heavenly Boaz invites us to intimate fellowship, too.

Scripture tells us, "Behold, I stand at the door and knock; if anyone hears and listens to and heeds My voice and opens the door, I will come in to him and will eat with him, and he [will eat] with Me" (Revelation 3:20 AMP). At this time of communion there is a deep exchange of life and love. This is a personal, intimate time in the fire of the passionate presence of Jesus.

When Ruth ate, she was sufficed, or satisfied and fulfilled. The apostle Paul says, "And He said unto me, My grace is sufficient for thee..." (2 Corinthians 12:9). I have heard an acronym for grace being "God's Riches And His Corresponding Empowerment." Yes, His divine presence and influence is more than enough!

Handfuls of Purpose!

And when she was risen up to glean, Boaz commanded his young men, saying, Let her glean even among the sheaves, and reproach her not: And let fall also some of the handfuls of purpose for her, and leave them, that she may glean them, and rebuke her not.
Ruth 2:15-16

Ruth was a diligent worker. She had a great work ethic and it was rewarded with favor. It reminds me of this passage, "Study to show thyself approved unto God, a workman who needeth not to be ashamed, rightly dividing the word of truth" (2 Timothy 2:15). Boaz expresses his approval by letting her gather as much as she possibly can. The Law only allowed foreigners to glean in the corner of the field but Grace lets her glean among the sheaves or in the midst of bunches of grain. We should declare with Paul, "Blessed be the God and Father of our Lord Jesus Christ, who hath blessed us with all spiritual blessings in heavenly places in Christ" (Ephesians 1:3).

Remember, Boaz is a type of Jesus who is full of grace and shows his excessive, extravagant love by leaving her "handfuls of purpose". When our Heavenly Boaz is involved in our life, there is abundance. Even today, look for and receive His abundant provision. Let us declare with the Psalmist David, "Blessed be the Lord, who daily loadeth us with benefits, even the God of our salvation. Selah" (Psalm 68:19). And "Selah" means stop and think about it.

A Workout

So she gleaned in the field until even, and beat out that she had gleaned: and it was about an ephah of barley. And she took it up, and went into the city: and her mother in law saw what she had gleaned: and she brought forth, and gave to her that she had reserved after she was sufficed.
Ruth 2:17-18

Scripture says, "... work out your own salvation with fear and trembling. For it is God which worketh in you both to will and to do of His good pleasure" (Philippians 2:12-13). Like Ruth, we are in a maturing process for more of the life of God operating in and through our lives. God blesses us so we have enough to give—whether it is in the spiritual or natural realm. We see that Ruth worked diligently when presented with an opportunity and favor.

Like God, Boaz gave her a large enough portion to bless not only herself, but also to share and to be a conduit of grace to others. We are "blessed to be a blessing."

Even so, when we are diligent in the Word of God, He will stir up within us scriptures which are just what is needed to bring life to someone in need. Stir yourself to be diligent in the Word, prayer and praise because you are to be used by God to supply to the Body of Christ. (Ephesians 4:16.)

Ruth is Preaching!

And her mother in law said unto her, Where hast thou
gleaned to day? and where wroughtest thou?
Blessed be he that did take knowledge of thee.
And she shewed her mother in law with whom
she had wrought, and said,
The man's name with whom I wrought today is Boaz.
Ruth 2:19

I can hear Naomi saying, "Where have you been?" And Ruth certainly has a testimony! It says she "shewed" Naomi with whom she had gleaned. This word in the Hebrew means to manifest; figuratively, to announce (always by word of mouth to one present); explain; praise; declare; expound;

messenger; profess; rehearse; report; shew (forth); speak; or, tell.

Ruth preached the good news of Boaz's love, grace, and favor to Naomi. Boaz, who is strength, wealth and joy, became the strength and joy of Ruth who in turn passed it along to Naomi. Ruth was able to communicate to Naomi that Boaz had blessed her beyond measure.

Boaz is Near of Kin

And Naomi said unto her daughter in law,
Blessed be he of the LORD, who hath not left off his
kindness to the living and to the dead.
And Naomi said unto her,
The man is near of kin unto us, one of our next kinsmen.
Ruth 2:20

The report keeps getting better and better! Naomi starts blessing God because she knew that Boaz was near of kin and was able to redeem all. The kinsman-redeemer is a picture of the Lord Jesus Christ. The term "kinsmen" in the Hebrew is *ga'al*, a primitive root meaning to redeem (according to the

Oriental law of kinship), i.e., to be the next of kin (and as such to buy back a relative's property, marry his widow etc.). There were three obligations of the kinsmen:

1. He was to redeem his brother and the property or inheritance of his brother.
2. He was to be the avenger for any fatal violence against his brother.
3. He was to raise up a successor for his brother. If a brother had died and had not left a son to be heir, the kinsmen-redeemer was to raise up seed for his brother.

This law operated in relation to the property, the person and posterity. Now, if the Law of Moses provided for redemption of the land, the widow, and future generations; what Christ has provided in the New Testament by His blood is better by far. Salvation by redemption is the greatest love story. Paul tells us, "Christ hath redeemed us from the curse of the law, being made a curse for us: for it is written, Cursed is every one that hangeth on a tree: That the blessing of Abraham might come on the Gentiles through Jesus Christ; that we might receive the promise of the Spirit through faith" (Galatians 3:13-14). We are positioned for incredible blessings. Hebrews 9:12 says, "Neither by the blood of goats and calves, but by his own blood he entered in once into the holy place, having obtained eternal redemption for us."

Our redeemer has provided for us everything necessary for abundant blessings, freedom, and fulfillment. Isaiah declares, "... Fear not: for I have redeemed thee, I have called thee by thy name; thou art Mine" (Isaiah 43:1). You are valued and loved; you have been redeemed by the precious blood of Jesus.

There is More! Say, "Harvest"!

And Ruth the Moabitess said, He said unto me also,
Thou shalt keep fast by my young men
until they have ended all my harvest.
Ruth 2:21

What does "the end of all my harvest" mean? Wikipedia defines harvest:

In agriculture, the harvest is the process of gathering mature crops from the fields. The harvest marks the end of the growing season, or the growing cycle for a particular crop, and this is the focus of seasonal celebrations of many religions.

In order for there to be a harvest, there must be fruit.

Boaz has a goal in mind and so does our heavenly Boaz. In our story this is a natural harvest of barley and wheat, but there is a supernatural, spiritual harvest being gathered by our Father. He is not settling for thirty or sixty percent but for complete fullness.

The whole harvest includes Jew and Greek, bond and free, and He is gathering all unto Himself. Paul explains, "Having made known unto us the mystery of His will, according to His good pleasure which He hath purposed in Himself: That in the dispensation of the fulness of times He might gather together in one all things in Christ, both which are in heaven, and which are on earth; even in Him" (Ephesians 1:9-10). God has great plans for you.

Let Patience Have
Her Perfect Work

And Naomi said unto Ruth her daughter in law,
It is good, my daughter, that thou go out with his maidens,
that they meet thee not in any other field. So she kept fast by the
maidens of Boaz to glean unto the end of barley harvest
and of wheat harvest; and dwelt with her mother in law.
Ruth 2:22-23

Now is the time to stay with the program until fullness. James shares, "So be patient, brethren, [as you wait] till the coming of the Lord. See how the farmer waits expectantly for the precious harvest from the land. [See how] he keeps up his patient [vigil] over it until it receives the early and late rains. So you also must be patient. Establish your hearts [strengthen and confirm them in the final certainty], for the coming of the Lord is very near" (James 5:7-8 AMP). These words were as applicable to Ruth as they are for us today.

Our husbandman is looking for fruit; the fruit that remains is love. God loves you and cares for you and wants to romance you and bring you into your purpose and destiny. Boaz was effective in cultivating a fruitful relationship with Ruth, and the Holy Spirit is successful with us. He leads us one step at a time. Let's keep in step!

Personal Application

- What has been a recent "hap" in your life? How has God orchestrated or ordered your steps?

- How do you see yourself possessing the promises God has given YOU?

- How are you positioning yourself to hear the voice of God?

- What scripture in this chapter meant the most to you? Why?

- Your Boaz has abundantly supplied you with handfuls of purpose. List a few and give Him thanks and praise!

Chapter 3

YOUR PREPARATORY
INSTRUCTIONS

Preparation is something I am familiar with both in the natural with sports and in the spiritual with the dealings of the Holy Spirit. Enduring grueling spring training with its repetition of plays for precise execution so that I would be prepared for the upcoming season was the price to pay for victory. The real game of life, which incorporates the eternal purpose of God in which we all have a significant role, requires our utmost participation, cooperation, preparation and discipline.

The Next Step

Then Naomi her mother in law said unto her,
My daughter, shall I not seek rest for thee,
that it may be well with thee?
Ruth 3:1

Previously the issue for Ruth and Naomi had been the need to quench the hunger pains of an empty stomach. Now that Boaz had supplied them so richly with grain, they moved on to the subject matter of "rest."

Rest is something we all seek. Jesus said, "Come unto Me, all ye that labour and are heavy laden, and I will give you rest" (Matthew 11:28). True rest is found in a personal relationship with Jesus, our heavenly Boaz. Jesus not only gives us rest but also desires intimate communion with us. "The LORD thy God in the midst of thee is mighty; He will save, He will rejoice over thee with joy; He will rest in

His love, He will joy over thee with singing" (Zephaniah 3:17).

And as we will see, Ruth was ready to go to the next level in this process of maturation.

Get to the Threshing floor

And now is not Boaz of our kindred
with whose maidens thou wast?
Behold, he winnoweth barley tonight in the threshing floor.
Ruth 3:2

Naomi's was the voice that advanced the unfolding purpose in the life of Ruth. Ruth has been submissive to the process, and it has served her well. She experienced the love of Boaz, and it was love that drew her where she needed to be.

The threshing floor is a painful but necessary place. What was to occur at the threshing floor that night was the "winnowing" of barley. *Winnow* means to separate the chaff from the grain by means of the current of air, to blow chaff off or away. Chaff is the outer hull that covers the grain as well as the straw of the stems and leaves. It is basically anything from the plants except the prized kernels of grain.

The time appointed—tonight—was the time of the increase of the flow of air in the natural. It was windier at night than in the day. Spiritually, it is the time of the wind of the Holy Spirit.

Even today, the wind of God is what separates the false or chaff from the genuine grain. Now is the time of the increase and filling afresh with the purity and power of Holy Spirit as happened to the early Church.

"And when the day of Pentecost was fully come, they were all with one accord in one place. And suddenly there came a sound from heaven as of a rushing mighty wind, and it filled all the house where they were sitting. And there appeared unto them cloven tongues like as of fire, and it sat upon each of them. And they were all filled with the Holy Ghost, and began to speak with other tongues, as the Spirit gave them utterance" (Acts 2:1-4).

Do you sense a fresh activity of the Holy Spirit? He is holy and that is why He is cleansing, purifying and removing what does not please Him, so that He can then fill us with more of His presence.

"Threshing floor" comes from a Hebrew word, *goren*, meaning to smooth. See, it is our threshing floor experience that removes irregularities and prepares us for a greater capacity of the presence of God. John the Baptist understood this. "I indeed baptize you in water unto repentance: but He that cometh after me is mightier than I, whose shoes I am not worthy to bear: He shall baptize you in the Holy Spirit and (in) fire: whose fan is in His hand, and He will thoroughly cleanse His threshing-floor; and He will gather His wheat into the garner, but the chaff He will burn up with unquenchable fire" (Matthew 3:11-12 ASV).

As the Holy Spirit smooths and sweeps us and fans away the chaff, it can be very uncomfortable. But He loves us too much to leave us in the condition we are in. In the context of the threshing floor experience, Isaiah sums up this experience, "The voice of one that crieth, Prepare ye in the wilderness the way of Jehovah; make level in the desert a highway for our God. Every valley shall be exalted, and every mountain and hill shall be made low; and the uneven shall be made level, and the rough places a plain: and the glory of Jehovah shall be revealed, and all flesh shall see it together; for the mouth of Jehovah hath spoken it" (Isaiah 40:3-5 ASV). The threshing floor was a necessary place for Ruth to go, and just as necessary for us, in order for the glory or purpose of God to be revealed.

Every time the threshing floor is mentioned in the Word, it presages an intensified encounter with the presence of God. This passage is no exception, "Then Solomon began to build the house of the LORD at Jerusalem in Mount Moriah, where the LORD appeared unto David his father, in the place that David had prepared in the threshing floor of Ornan the Jebusite" (2 Chronicles 3:1).

For the history of the threshing floor of Ornan see 2 Samuel 24:14-25 and 1 Chronicles 21:15-28. King David (the Father) prepared the threshing floor so Solomon (his son) could build the house of the Lord there. Likewise, our Father has made all the necessary preparations, including our redemption, so the house of the Lord within our hearts is built. When Solomon's temple was completed, the glory of God filled that temple. The dedication of Solomon's Temple in 2 Chronicles 5 is a tremendous picture of what happened thousands of years ago, but it is also exactly what God wants in our lives at our threshing floor. "So that the priests could not stand to minister by reason of the cloud: for the glory of the LORD had filled the house of God" (2 Chronicles 5:14).

Yes, he wants to fill you with his glory and manifest presence! Remember, the reason for the threshing floor experience is to release the grain from the husks and chaff. "When Christ, (who is) our life, shall be manifested, then shall ye also with Him be manifested in glory" (Colossians 3:4 ASV).

Ruth Follows Four Instructions

Wash thyself therefore, and anoint thee, and put thy raiment upon thee, and get thee down to the floor: but make not thyself known unto the man, until he shall have done eating and drinking.
Ruth 3:3

Bishop Rick Thomas says, "The instructions you are willing to follow today will determine your future." This could not be more evident than in the life and destiny of Ruth. Because she was willing to follow Naomi's instructions, she ended up in the lineage of the Messiah, Jesus Christ. Certainly we can learn much from her example.

Following these four instructions would be wise for all of us:

1. Wash Thyself.

We are to be washed by being immersed in the life of God. The Word is Spirit and life, and the Word is a person. As you read these scriptures, the Spirit will operate and do a special work in you:

> *Husbands, love your wives, even as Christ also loved the church, and gave himself for it;*
> *That he might sanctify and cleanse it with the washing of water by the word, That he might present it to himself a glorious church, not having spot, or wrinkle, or any such thing; but that it should be holy and without blemish.*
> *Ephesians 5:25-27*

> *In the beginning was the Word, and the Word was with God, and the Word was God.*
> *John 1:1*

> *And the Word was made flesh, and dwelt among us, (and we beheld his glory, the glory as*

*of the only begotten of the Father,) full of grace
and truth.*
John 1:14

*Sanctify them through thy truth: thy word is
truth.*
John 17:17

*Let us draw near with a true heart in full assur-
ance of faith, having our hearts sprinkled from
an evil conscience, and our bodies washed with
pure water.*
Hebrews 10:22

*. . . Unto him that loved us, and washed us from
our sins in his own blood.*
Revelation 1:5

2. Get Anointed

Just as the Word is a person, the Anointing is a person. *Messiah* in Hebrew and *Christ* in Greek both
mean anointed or the anointed one.

*Now he who establishes us with you in Christ
and has anointed us is God.*
2 Corinthians 1:21 NKJV

...and the yoke shall be destroyed because of the
anointing.
Isaiah 10:27

The Spirit of the Lord is upon me, because he
hath anointed me to preach the gospel to the
poor; he hath sent me to heal the brokenhearted,
to preach deliverance to the captives, and recov-
ering of sight to the blind, to set at liberty them
that are bruised.
Luke 4:18

How God anointed Jesus of Nazareth with the
Holy Ghost and with power: who went about
doing good, and healing all that were oppressed
of the devil; for God was with him.
Acts 10:38

Thou hast loved righteousness, and hated iniqui-
ty; therefore God, even thy God, hath anointed
thee with the oil of gladness above thy fellows.
Hebrews 1:9

But the anointing which ye have received of him
abideth in you, and ye need not that any man
teach you: but as the same anointing teacheth
you of all things, and is truth, and is no lie, and
even as it hath taught you, ye shall abide in
him.
1 John 2:27

Exodus 30 lists the ingredients of the holy anointing oil, which are ingredients that are to be operating in our lives.

> *Moreover the LORD spake unto Moses, saying, Take thou also unto thee principal spices, of pure <u>myrrh</u> five hundred shekels, and of sweet <u>cinnamon</u> half so much, even two hundred and fifty shekels, and of sweet <u>calamus</u> two hundred and fifty shekels, And of <u>cassia</u> five hundred shekels, after the shekel of the sanctuary, and of <u>oil olive</u> an hin: And thou shalt make it an oil of holy ointment, an ointment compound after the art of the apothecary: it shall be an holy anointing oil.*
> Exodus 30:22-25

There are five ingredients of the Oil of Holy Ointment:

- **Pure Myrrh.** "Pure" in Hebrew means to move rapidly, liberty, a flowing, to run free. When we have a pure heart, there is the ability to flow. Paul writes, "Now the Lord is that Spirit: and where the Spirit of the Lord is, there is liberty"

(2 Corinthians 3:17). And, Jesus said, "Blessed are the pure in heart for they shall see God" (Matthew 5:8).

Myrrh in Hebrew means bitterness or bitter. Scripture says, "... if so be that we suffer with him, that we may be also glorified together. For I reckon that the sufferings of this present time are not worthy to be compared with the glory which shall be revealed in us" (Romans 8:17-18).

- **Sweet Cinnamon.** The Hebrew word is from a now-unused root word meaning to erect, referring to upright rolls of cinnamon bark. The bark of the cinnamon tree is stripped off and rolled. Scripture says, "... but the upright shall have good things in possession" (Proverbs 28:10).

- **Sweet Calamus.** In Hebrew this word means a reed (as upright), resembling a rod (especially one used for measuring), a shaft, stem, balance, bone, branch, and cane. A rod in scripture speaks of authority. The standard of measurement is the nature of Christ. In the Hebrew definition we see depicted the shaft and branch. These point to the candlestick—the lampstand described in Exodus 25:31-37, which had a central shaft declaring the preeminence of the Lord Jesus Christ, who is the light of the world. He is the vine and we are the branches.

- **Cassia.** Similar to the cinnamon tree, cassia in Hebrew comes from a primitive root, meaning to shrivel up, i.e., to contract or bend the body (or neck) in deference: bow (down) (the) head, to stoop. When you bow your head, you are bowing the neck or your will. This represents the surrendered life of true humility and worship.

- **Oil Olive.** It is the Holy Spirit that activates and releases all the ingredients to flow together. All anointing flows out of the Anointed One, and we are called to anoint the Head, Jesus Christ with our worship. This psalm of love sums it up: "Thou hast loved righteousness, and hated wickedness: therefore God, thy God, hath anointed thee with the oil of gladness above thy fellows. All thy garments (smell of) myrrh, and aloes, (and) cassia; out of ivory palaces stringed instruments have made thee glad" (Psalm 45:7-8 ASV).

3. Get Clothed.

Clothing is first mentioned in the Garden of Eden. "Unto Adam also and to his wife did the LORD God make coats of skins, and clothed them" (Genesis 3:21). This is when they were naked and ashamed and the Lord covered them. This action of the Lord's foreshadows our being covered by the blood of the Savior—the slain Lamb of God. In the process of changing our garments, God brings us to the cross and presents to us the Lamb who was slain from the foundation of the world (Revelation 13:8).

I will greatly rejoice in the LORD, my soul shall be joyful in my God; for he hath clothed me with the garments of salvation, he hath covered me with the robe of righteousness, as a bridegroom decketh himself with ornaments, and as a bride adorneth herself with her jewels.
Isaiah 61:10

The king's daughter is all glorious within: her clothing is of wrought gold.
Psalm 45:13

She is not afraid of the snow for her household:
for all her household are clothed with scarlet.
Proverbs 31:21

And behold, I send forth the promise of my Fa-
ther upon you: but tarry ye in the city, until ye
be clothed with power from on high.
Luke 24:49 ASV

Likewise, ye younger, submit yourselves unto the
elder. Yea, all of you be subject one to another,
and be clothed with humility: for God resisteth
the proud, and giveth grace to the humble.
1 Peter 5:5

Wherefore take unto you the whole armour of
God, that ye may be able to withstand in the
evil day, and having done all, to stand. Stand
therefore, having your loins girt about with
truth, and having on the breastplate of right-
eousness; And your feet shod with the prepara-
tion of the gospel of peace; Above all, taking the
shield of faith, wherewith ye shall be able to
quench all the fiery darts of the wicked. And
take the helmet of salvation, and the sword of the
Spirit, which is the word of God.
Ephesians 6:13-17

And that, knowing the time, that now it is high
time to awake out of sleep: for now is our salva-

tion nearer than when we believed. The night is far spent, the day is at hand: let us therefore cast off the works of darkness, and let us put on the armour of light. Let us walk honestly, as in the day; not in rioting and drunkenness, not in chambering and wantonness, not in strife and envying. But put ye on the Lord Jesus Christ, and make not provision for the flesh, to fulfil the lusts thereof.
Romans 13:11-14

Awake, awake; put on thy strength, O Zion; put on thy beautiful garments, O Jerusalem, the holy city: for henceforth there shall no more come into thee the uncircumcised and the unclean.
Isaiah 52:1

Let us be glad and rejoice, and give honour to him: for the marriage of the Lamb is come, and his wife hath made herself ready. And to her was granted that she should be arrayed in fine linen, clean and white: for the fine linen is the righteousness of saints.
Revelation 19:7-8

4. Get to the Threshing Floor.

It took faith for Ruth to be properly aligned and in agreement with her purpose. She was in harmony with the Word; she smelled good and had a sweet sound of praise and worship. Wow! What next?

Personal Application

- Are you aware of the preparatory work of the Holy Spirit in your life? What is the Holy Spirit speaking to you?

- List the important instructions given to Ruth by Naomi to prepare her for her life changing encounter with Boaz at the threshing floor. How can you apply this to your own life?

Chapter 4

WHAT DO YOU SEE?

I n chapter one Ruth left Moab, she was saved, and demonstrated a willingness to move forward. She was properly positioned at the right place at the right time with the right people. God is no respecter of persons. What He did for Ruth, He wants for you, and more! Now let us turn our attention to Boaz to understand more.

Mark the Ark

And it shall be, when he lieth down,
that thou shalt mark the place where he shall lie,
and thou shalt go in, and uncover his feet, and lay thee
down; and he will tell thee what thou shalt do.
And she said unto her, All that thou sayest unto me I
will do. And she went down unto the floor, and did ac-
cording to all that her mother in law bade her.
Ruth 3:4-6

We see in Ruth a submissive, willing heart that learns and receives instructions from Naomi. May we have the same surrendered heart. Quoting Bishop Rick Thomas, "The instructions you are willing to obey today will create the future you will have. God always meets a need with instructions."

Truth is timeless. As we read in Proverbs, "Hear instruction, and be wise, and refuse it not. Blessed is the man that heareth me, watching daily at my gates, waiting at the posts of my doors. For whoso findeth me findeth life, and shall obtain favour of the LORD" (Proverbs 8:33-35). As we watch, hear and obey we ultimately find life. What a promise!

Ruth was to mark the place where Boaz slept. Her eyes were to be focused on the goal. I can identify with this from my basketball days. In order to score and hear the sound of the "swish" that meant you had made it, I learned to focus my vision on the rim of the basketball hoop. I still hold the State of Florida high school record for points scored! But, more importantly, we need to keep our attention on Jesus.

"Where there is no vision, the people cast off restraint; But he that keepeth the law, happy is he" (Proverbs 29:18 ASV). So where there is vision, there is self-control, discipline, and an understanding of Jesus' purposes for our lives. A disciple is a disciplined one who has his eye on the prize as Paul did: "I press toward the mark for the prize of the high calling of God in Christ Jesus" (Philippians 3:14). What are we running towards? Where are we investing our energies, emotions, and thought-life? Are we enhancing and serving the progressive vision of God?

In the Old Testament the Israelites were instructed to "keep their eye" on the ark. Listen to their directives, " And they commanded the people, saying, When ye **see the ark** of the covenant of the LORD your God, and the priests the Levites bearing it, then ye shall remove from your place, and go after it. Yet there shall be a space between you and it, about two thousand cubits by measure: come not near unto it, that ye may know the way by which ye must go: for ye have not passed this way heretofore. And Joshua said unto the people, Sanctify yourselves: for tomorrow the LORD will do wonders among you" (Joshua 3:3-5). The "ark" is a type of Jesus Christ and His glorious, triumphant, victorious life. It speaks of the manifest presence of the reigning King of kings and Lord of lords.

Just as Ruth was to mark the place and the Israelites were to mark the Ark of the Covenant, we today must mark the "Ark"! When our thoughts are on His complete victory over every foe, and when we realize that because of His triumph we are victorious also, there is freedom. Jesus said, "... It is finished: and He bowed His head, and gave up the ghost" (John 19:30). We need to enter into what He has provided.

Go In, Ruth!

We can look at something all day but if we do not actively participate, we will not be part of the program. If we do not make it personal we are living in a fairy tale. Ruth's next step was to go in. God wants us to have intimacy with Him, to come up close and personal. We have access to the very presence of God! The veil of separation was ripped open by the death of Jesus. The veil of the temple was rent from top to bottom when he died on the cross. "Having therefore, brethren, boldness to enter into the holiest by the blood of Jesus, By a new and living way, which he hath consecrated for us, through the veil, that is to say, his flesh" (Hebrews 10:19-20).

Paul instructs us, "Let us therefore come boldly unto the throne of grace, that we may obtain mercy, and find grace to help in time of need" (Hebrews 4:16). And, notice that it is a place of mercy and grace!

Ruth's submissive attitude, demonstrated by taking a position at Boaz's feet, reveals her surrendered heart. She made a bold move to be at the threshing floor, and she entrusted her future into his hands. Her actions brought Boaz to the place of decision to fulfill his duty as the kinsman.

Uncover His Feet?

And when Boaz had eaten and drunk, and his heart was merry,
he went to lie down at the end of the heap of corn: and
she came softly, and uncovered his feet, and laid her down.
Ruth 3:7

Once again, Ruth was actively involved. Faith played an active role in the journey. Mountains are not going to move by themselves! God wants our participation. She uncovered Boaz's feet as Naomi had instructed. You can be sure that this has important spiritual significance. If one "uncovers" something, discovery is implied. And, yes, we have some finding out to do.

There are depths in Christ that we need to ascertain by His Spirit. I love the Word because in it I discover The Author. Not only do I become intimately acquainted with The Father, I also get to know myself. Scripture says, "That they all may be one; as thou, Father, art in me, and I in thee, that they also may be one in us: that the world may believe that thou hast sent me. And the glory which thou gavest me I have given them; that they may be one, even as we are one: I in them, and thou in me, that they may be made perfect in one; and that the world may know that thou hast sent me, and hast loved them, as thou hast loved me" (John 17:21-23).

This is powerful! The world will not believe until we believe and come to a place where we know our union or oneness with The Father. So what is so important about "uncovering the feet?"

In Isaiah we see the "feet" announcing peace. "How beautiful upon the mountains are the feet of him that bringeth good tidings, that publisheth peace; that bringeth good tidings of good, that publisheth salvation; that saith unto Zion, Thy God reigneth!" (Isaiah 52:7).

Jesus was and is the good news, but now look: "And how shall they preach, except they be sent? as it is written, How beautiful are the feet of them that preach the gospel of peace, and bring glad tidings of good things!" (Romans 10:15).

As we discover the good news of the gospel, we become one with it and bring glad tidings to the world in which we live. As Ruth uncovered Boaz' feet, her purpose becomes clearer. Listen to the understanding Isaiah had about the feet. "The glory of Lebanon shall come unto thee, the fir tree, the pine tree, and the box together, to beautify the place of my sanctuary; and I will make the place of my feet glorious" (Isaiah 60:13).

We are His sanctuary, the people who have been beautified by His presence, light, glory, and love. You are beautiful!

The Place of God's Glorious Throne

The Prophet Ezekiel also had an awesome revelation about the "feet":

> And the glory of the LORD came into the house by the way of the gate whose prospect is toward the east. So the spirit took me up, and brought me into the inner court; and, behold, the glory of the LORD filled the house. And I heard him speaking unto me out of the house; and the man stood by me. And he said unto me, Son of man, the place of my throne, and the place of

*the soles of my feet, where I will dwell in the midst of
the children of Israel for ever,
and my holy name...*
Ezekiel 43:4-7

The place of God's throne is in the midst of a "feet company." Notice the "feet of him" in Isaiah 52:7, becomes the "feet of them" in Romans 10:15. I use the term "feet company," as do others in that the "feet" indicate establishing possession of a location or territory. It is a symbol of taking possession and extending the purposes of God in the earth.

Now for the punch line: "For You have put everything in subjection under his feet. Now in putting everything in subjection to man, He left nothing outside [of man's] control. But at present we do not yet see all things subjected to him [man]. But we are able to see Jesus..." (Hebrews 2:8-9 AMP).

As we keep our eyes on Jesus—the Ark who secured the victory—we, the glorious feet, will follow in triumph.

The feet have a function, but they must move with the Ark!

*Behold, the ark of the covenant of the Lord of all the
earth passeth over before you into Jordan. Now therefore take you twelve men out of the tribes of Israel, out
of every tribe a man. And it shall come to pass, as soon
as the soles of the feet of the priests that bear the ark of
the LORD, the Lord of all the earth, shall rest in the
waters of Jordan, that the waters of Jordan shall be cut
off from the waters that come down from above; and
they shall stand upon an heap. And it came to pass,
when the people removed from their tents, to pass over
Jordan, and the priests bearing the ark of the covenant
before the people; And as they that bare the ark were
come unto Jordan, and the feet of the priests that bare
the ark were dipped in the brim of the water, (for Jordan overfloweth all his banks all the time of harvest,)
That the waters which came down from above stood
and rose up upon an heap very far from the city Adam, that is beside Zaretan: and those that came down
toward the sea of the plain, even the salt sea, failed,
and were cut off: and the people passed over right
against Jericho. And the priests that bare the ark of the
covenant of the LORD stood firm on dry ground in
the midst of Jordan, and all the Israelites passed over
on dry ground, until all the people were passed clean
over Jordan.*

Joshua 3:11-17

Notice that the "feet company" had to move for the Jordan to be stopped. *Jordan* in Hebrew means "descender." The Israelites were the ones to put the downward pull of death under their feet. At a time when the Jordan was overflowing its banks, there was a miracle!

Just when all hell is breaking loose, we see a miracle. That is why we cannot keep our focus on the temporal circumstances. We must "mark the Ark." Sometimes, when our circumstances appear the bleakest or most chaotic, that is when God steps in by His supernatural power.

When the bearers of the Ark of the Covenant stepped into the Jordan, the waters split. When Jesus stepped into the "waters of death," He conquered death, hell, and the grave. This account in Joshua is a prophetic picture that the Church will also experientially possess His victory two thousand years later.

Jesus Christ, the Ark, has cut off every hindrance all the way back to Adam. Paul says it this way, " For as in Adam all die, even so in Christ shall all be made alive" (1 Corinthians 15:22). The secret entrance to Kingdom living is through our Ark— the victorious, resurrected life of Jesus Christ.

Your Feet Have Been Washed

The Father has provided for our every need so that we can be what He has called us to be on the earth. John records the washing of the disciple's feet at the Last Supper. "So after he had washed their feet, and had taken his garments, and was set down again, he said unto them, Know ye what I have done to you? Ye call me Master and Lord: and ye say well; for so I am. If I then, your Lord and Master, have washed your feet; ye also ought to wash one another's feet. For I have given you an example, that ye should do as I have done to you" (John 13:12-15).

Jesus declares, "Now ye are clean through the word which I have spoken unto you" (John 15:3). Being in contact with the world distracts us from the reality of who we are in Christ and our mission on the earth. So He washed their feet to cleanse off all defilement.

His Feet were Anointed

"There they made him a supper; and Martha served: but Lazarus was one of them that sat at the table with him. Then took Mary a pound of ointment of spikenard, very costly, and anointed the feet of Jesus, and wiped his feet with her hair: and the house was filled with the odour of the ointment. Then saith one of his disciples, Judas Iscariot, Simon's son, which should betray him, Why was not this ointment sold for three hundred pence, and given to the poor?" (John 12:2-5).

We are living in the day of the unveiling of the "feet company," the part of the body in contact with the earth. And, prophetically, this company has had applied to it costly anointment.

Spikenard is precious and costly. The Greek translation of spikenard sheds incredible light. Strong's definition tells us that spikenard is derived from *pistis*; meaning trustworthy, genuine (unadulterated): persuasion, credence; moral conviction (of religious truth, or the truthfulness of God or a religious teacher), especially reliance upon Christ for salvation; assurance, belief, faith.

The "feet company" has been anointed to be full of belief and faith. The "odour" that filled the house is the same smell that fills our house with faith, confidence, and belief. Jesus asked a poignant question, "... Nevertheless, when the Son of man cometh, shall he find faith on the earth?" (Luke 18:8). Notice that it is when He comes, not when the saints go.

Peter writes, "... to them that have obtained like precious faith with us through the righteousness of God and our Savior Jesus Christ" (2 Peter 1:1). Our Father's purpose will be done on earth through His faith, love, and anointing. It is the finished work of Jesus on Calvary that paid the price and made it possible.

Anointed for Victory

Scripture says, "For he must reign, till he hath put all enemies under his feet. The last enemy that shall be destroyed is death. For he hath put all things under his feet. But when he saith, all things are put under him, it is manifest that he is excepted, which did put all things under him. And when all things shall be subdued unto him, then shall the Son also himself be subject unto him that put all things under him, that God may be all in all" (1 Corinthians 15:25-28). He is expecting success and victory. What a wonderful plan of redemption! "For whatsoever is born of God overcometh the world: and this is the victory that overcometh the world, even our faith. Who is he that overcometh the world, but he that believeth that Jesus is the Son of God?" (1 John 5:4-5).

Another scripture regarding this feet company is penned by David, "It is God that girdeth me with strength, and maketh my way perfect. He maketh my feet like hinds' feet, and setteth me upon my high places" (Psalm 18:32-33). These high places are in the realms of spirit and truth where we are now seated. The higher we are, the farther we can see.

Ruth has been in the presence of Boaz and she was awakening. Since her transition, she was losing all contact and connection with Moab and was beginning to live and move and have her being, identity, focus, and faith in God alone. Let us mark Him and the place where He has lain down. That is the finished work of Jesus Christ!

There may be areas or situations in your life that are difficult, but know this, "… all things work together for good to them that love God, to them who are the called according to his purpose" (Romans 8:28). With the help of His Spirit God wants you to rise above every circumstance. In the face of difficulty, "Mark the Ark," the victorious life of Jesus Christ. Then you will soar on the wings of an eagle in God's glorious presence.

Personal Application

- How have you marked the ARK?

- What are you seeing or perceiving from the Holy Spirit?

- What faith declarations of the Lordship of Jesus do you want to announce that He reigns over in your life?

- What is your understanding of the "feet company?"

Chapter 5

WHAT ARE YOU WAITING FOR? He is the Author & the Finisher!

Decisions to move forward are not always easy. It is difficult to move forward when you are in the land of the unknown, where you do not have a sure footing. This is especially true if you prefer the familiar and well-defined pathway.

Many times the ways of faith are dark and un-tried, but a pioneer must blaze new trails to gain new territory. Observe what the officers empha-sized to the Israelites as they left the wilderness and entered into the Promised Land: ".... for ye have not passed this way heretofore" (Joshua 3:4).

It is Dark at Midnight

And it came to pass at midnight, that the man was afraid, and turned himself: and, behold, a woman lay at his feet.
Ruth 3:8

Midnight reveals a transitional time when it is in-tensely dark. At midnight Paul and Silas were in a jail; they praised God and were released. In Mat-thew 25:1-13, Jesus shares a parable that happened at midnight:

Then shall the kingdom of heaven be likened unto ten virgins, which took their lamps, and went forth to meet the bridegroom. And five of them were wise, and five were foolish. They that were foolish took their lamps, and took no oil with them: But the wise took oil in their vessels with their lamps. While the bride-groom tarried, they all slumbered and slept. And at midnight there was a cry made, Behold, the bridegroom cometh; go ye out to meet him. Then all those virgins arose, and trimmed their lamps. And the foolish said unto the wise, Give us of your oil; for our lamps are gone out. But the wise answered, saying, Not so; lest there be not enough for us and you: but go ye rather to them that sell, and buy for yourselves.

And while they went to buy, the bridegroom came; and they that were ready went in with him to the marriage: and the door was shut. Afterward came also the other virgins, saying, Lord, Lord, open to us. But he answered and said, Verily I say unto you, I know you not. Watch therefore, for ye know neither the day nor the hour wherein the Son of Man cometh.

The heralder who made the midnight cry to go meet the bridegroom was the mature, prepared one we should emulate. Obviously, he had an ear to hear and he was encouraging others to go out and meet the bridegroom.

Ruth had her midnight hour and so do we. She was pressing in to claim her possessions and she was getting attention. Ruth's actions remind me of Paul's purpose. "Brethren, I count not myself to have apprehended: but this one thing I do, forgetting those things which are behind, and reaching forth unto those things which are before, I press toward the mark for the prize of the high calling of

God in Christ Jesus" (Philippians 3:13-14). It is time to press on and go out to meet Him.

Who Are YOU?

And he said, Who art thou? And she answered, I am Ruth thine handmaid: spread therefore thy skirt over thine handmaid, for thou art a near kinsman.
Ruth 3:9

This is a covenantal term meaning what relationship do you have with me? Ruth had come to understand who she was. Identity determines destiny; therefore, we can not afford to have a mistaken identity. Ruth's former identity, or point of reference, was Moab. Now, however, she had found a place of security. She responded correctly. She was not intimidated by her past, nor was she living in shame or fear. She realized her background; ancestry or natural heritage did not matter. She had discovered the truth of Paul's revelation: "Therefore if any man be in Christ, he is a new creature: old things are passed away; behold, all things are become new" (2 Corinthians 5:17).

Her answer to the question was bold, confident and convincing. She uncovered her true purpose and identity. There was another lady who understood her value, worth and significance: the Shulamite woman in the Song of Songs. Her confession is similar: "I am my beloved's, and his desire is toward me" (Song 7:10). When you declare, "I am thine," you know you are bought with a price.

Paul shares, "What? know ye not that your body is the temple of the Holy Ghost which is in you, which ye have of God, and ye are not your own? For ye are bought with a price: therefore glorify God in your body, and in your spirit, which are God's" (1 Corinthians 6:19-20). The precious blood of the Lamb redeemed you. Know that you are valued and loved and created for a purpose. "Herein is our love made perfect, that we may have boldness in the day of judgment: because as he is, so are we in this world" (1 John 4:17). As we know we are to be like Him, we can say with Jesus, "Then said I, Lo, I come (in the volume of the book it is written of me,) to do thy will, O God" (Hebrews 10:7). This should be our testimony: "I come to do thy will; I am your handmaiden."

Similarly to Jesus and Ruth, you have a script that has already been preplanned, preprogrammed, predestined that you are to live out. Your story was in the mind of God before you put on your earth suit. The end was already established from the beginning. "Declaring the end from the beginning, and from ancient times the things that are not yet done, saying, My counsel shall stand, and I will do all my pleasure" (Isaiah 46:10).

When we know the way has been made, we can approach Him with confidence. Ruth is boldly asking for Boaz to be her kinsman-redeemer.

The prophet Ezekiel shares a similar scene: "Now when I passed by thee, and looked upon thee, behold, thy time was the time of love; and I spread my skirt over thee, and covered thy nakedness: yea, I sware unto thee, and entered into a covenant with thee, saith the Lord GOD, and thou becamest mine" (Ezekiel 16:8).

This was Ruth's time or season of love. After all, the object and purpose of the workings of God is our union with Him. "But God, who is rich in mercy, for his great love wherewith he loved us, Even when we were dead in sins, hath quickened us together with Christ, (by grace ye are saved;) And hath raised us up together, and made us sit together in heavenly places in Christ Jesus" (Ephesians 2:4-6).

Fear Not!

And now, my daughter, fear not; I will do to thee all that thou requirest: for all the city of my people doth know that thou art a virtuous woman.
Ruth 3:11

Fear was a major roadblock in my life. I feared surrendering my life to Christ, feared speaking in front of people, feared not being accepted, feared I was inadequate, and on and on. At the church I grew up in, Sunday night service included testimony time. The thought of standing in front of all those people was petrifying. Another one of my fears was that God would send me to Africa as a missionary.

Through my relationship with Jesus profound changes have occurred, one of which was overcoming the fear of public speaking. The more His love saturated me and became alive within me, the more I was compelled to share. I wanted others to experience His presence. Never would I have imagined the joy it would bring me to preach in the nations including the Philippines, South America, and Nicaragua. I am sure Africa is on God's agenda for me, as well! "For God hath not given us the spirit of fear; but of power, and of love, and of a sound mind" (2 Timothy 1:7).

I Will!

"And my God will liberally supply (fill to the full) your every need according to His riches in glory in Christ Jesus" (Philippians 4:19 AMP). Yes, God is a good God; He loves you and He wants to bless you!

I Know!

Ruth has come a long way; even the city knows of her virtue. God's grace has been sufficient. "Who can find a virtuous woman? for her price is far above rubies" (Proverbs 31:10). This word "virtuous" has the exact same meaning as "wealth" used to describe

Boaz in Ruth 2:1. "Virtuous" comes from a Hebrew word *chayil* meaning army, man of valor, valiant, power, ability, riches, substance and from *chuwl* which means pained, form, travail, dance, calve, to bring forth. This applies to Ruth and to you and me—virtuous ones bringing forth the nature of Christ. Our Boaz, Jesus Christ, is our mighty man of wealth and has the ability to bring forth His nature and character within us.

Who is This Nearer Kinsman?

And now it is true that I am thy near kinsman:
howbeit there is a kinsman nearer than I.
Ruth 3:12

This kinsman, a relative who was closer in relationship than Boaz, represents the Law, the very thing which Jesus dealt with. "For the law of the Spirit of life in Christ Jesus hath made me free from the law of sin and death. For what the law could not do, in that it was weak through the flesh, God sending his own Son in the likeness of sinful flesh, and for sin, condemned sin in the flesh" (Romans 8:2-3).

As we will see, the nearer kinsman (the Law) could not and did not want to perform the part of a kinsman. He really only wanted the land and to protect himself. He did not desire Ruth, nor did he want to raise up seed for her dead husband. The Law is selfish and self-serving.

A Long Night;
Who Likes to Wait?

Tarry this night, and it shall be in the morning, that if he will perform unto thee the part of a kinsman, well; let him do the kinsman's part: but if he will not do the part of a kinsman to thee, then will I do the part of a kinsman to thee, as the LORD liveth: lie down until the morning.
Ruth 3:13

Ruth's request was for marriage and Boaz's answer was, "I will do all you require" (v. 11). Wow!

But now, Ruth had to wait. Sometimes the hardest thing to do is to sit still.

I understand waiting. I waited 20 years for God to answer my prayer for a husband. But, in looking back, I am so thankful. I had to change before God could join me with the one He had planned for me.

At times I thought my answer would never manifest, but miracles do happen! The saying, "All good things come to those that wait," was true for me. For you who are waiting for your miracle, perhaps Psalm 40:1-3 is a promise you can stand on.

Morning is coming for you, just like it did for Ruth, and just like it did for the Shulamite woman in the Song of Solomon. "Until the day break, and the shadows flee away, turn, my beloved, and be thou like a roe or a young hart upon the mountains of Bether" (Song 2:17). The day is breaking, the shadows, veils, and slumber flee away as we follow His leading.

Good Morning to You

And she lay at his feet until the morning: and she rose
up before one could know another. And he said, Let it
not be known that a woman came into the floor.
Ruth 3:14

Ruth lay at His feet until the morning. She had to come to an even deeper level of trusting in Boaz's protection, because for her to be found there at midnight would have meant certain disgrace in the eyes of the Law. But, grace trumps the Law any day!

Another interesting event happened "in the morning" from which we can learn a great deal.

And it shall come to pass, that the man's rod, whom I shall choose, shall blossom: and I will make to cease from me the murmurings of the children of Israel, whereby they murmur against you. And Moses spake unto the children of Israel, and every one of their princes gave him a rod apiece, for each prince one, according to their fathers' houses, even twelve rods: and the rod of Aaron was among their rods. And Moses laid up the rods before the LORD in the tabernacle of witness.

And it came to pass, that on the morrow Moses went into the tabernacle of witness; and, behold,

the rod of Aaron for the house of Levi was budded, and brought forth buds, and bloomed blossoms, and yielded almonds.

Numbers 17:5-8

This was a miracle, a dry stick producing a harvest of almonds overnight! God is the same yesterday, today and forever. What are you believing for? What are you seeing? Ruth saw her kinsman-redeemer as her groom.

Jeremiah the prophet provides some assistance: "Moreover the word of the LORD came unto me, saying, 'Jeremiah, what seest thou?' And I said, 'I see a rod of an almond tree.' Then said the LORD unto me, 'Thou hast well seen: for I will hasten my word to perform it'" (Jeremiah 1:11-12). As soon as Jeremiah saw the branch of the almond tree, God moved to perform, execute, accomplish and fulfill what He had shown him. The Word says, "The LORD will perfect that which concerneth me: Thy mercy, O LORD, endureth for ever..." (Psalm 138:8).

Provision Until The Promise is Obtained

Also he said, Bring the veil that thou hast upon thee, and hold it. And when she held it, he measured six measures of barley, and laid it on her: and she went in-to the city.
Ruth 3:15

When we bring our vessel to God in obedience, He fills it to capacity. Remember, previously Ruth labored in the field all day and she gleaned just one measure. Now she was no longer living on leftovers. She was living in the overflow. Boaz added six measures to her one. Now she had seven, the number of completion, perfection and fullness. It is grace upon grace that he lavishly bestows. Scripture declares, "For out of His fullness (abundance) we have all received [all had a share and we were all supplied with] one grace after another and spiritual blessing upon spiritual blessing and even favor upon favor and gift [heaped] upon gift" (John 1:16 AMP).

Grace and Glory

And when she came to her mother in law, she said,
Who art thou, my daughter? And she told her all that
the man had done to her. And she said, These six
measures of barley gave he me; for he said to me,
Go not empty unto thy mother in law.
Ruth 3:16-17

Ruth's countenance was so visibly changed that her mother-in-law asked, "Who are you?" That is what the presence of the Lord does to us. The love, generosity, provision, and protection that are found in His presence visibly change us when we spend time with Him.

> *For the LORD God is a sun and shield;*
> *The LORD will give grace and glory;*
> *No good thing will He withhold*
> *From those who walk uprightly.*
> *O LORD of hosts,*
> *Blessed is the man who trusts in You!*
> *Psalm 84:11-12 NKJV*

Ruth was bubbling over with the good news and the provision she had to share with Naomi! We, too, never go away empty-handed from God's presence or with just enough for ourselves. There is always good news to share.

The gospel is good news. "And this gospel of the kingdom shall be preached in all the world for a witness unto all nations; and then shall the end come" (Matthew 24:14). God wants the whole world to know of His love, blessings and provision. God has given us specific "assignments"—the Naomis for whom we have been strategically positioned to reach with the blessings of life.

Finishing Faith

Then said she, Sit still, my daughter, until thou know
how the matter will fall: for the man will not be in rest
until he have finished the thing this day.
Ruth 3:18

Ruth, who by virtue of her birth in Moab did not have a goodly heritage, has now been accepted. The Psalmist David explains, "The lines are fallen unto me in pleasant places; yea, I have a goodly heritage" (Psalm 16:6).

Our heritage is great in Christ! No matter our background, once we come to Christ, our Kinsman-redeemer, our heritage is assured!

We can rest in strength and certainty in the truth of God's Word. "Being confident of this very thing, that he which hath begun a good work in you will perform it until the day of Jesus Christ" (Philippians 1:6).

Personal Application

- Are you willing and committed to be at the feet of Jesus in your midnight hour?

- Based on God's Word, *who* are you?

- What do you sense is *your* assignment in relation to the command from Boaz in Ruth 3:7: "Go ye not empty handed"?

Chapter 6

LOVE MAKES ALL THINGS POSSIBLE

In the love chapter written by the Apostle Paul he shares that Love "beareth all things, believeth all things, hopeth all things, endureth all things. Charity never faileth: ... And now abideth faith, hope, charity, these three; but the greatest of these is charity" (1 Corinthians 13:7-8,13).

When I was a little girl, my Mom gave me ten dollars when I memorized this chapter. It means so much more to me now, more than ever.

Love Acts

Then went Boaz up to the gate, and sat him down there: and, behold, the kinsman of whom Boaz spake came by; unto whom he said, Ho, such a one! turn aside, sit down here. And he turned aside, and sat down. And he took ten men of the elders of the city, and said, Sit ye down here. And they sat down. And he said unto the kinsman, Naomi, that is come again out of the country of Moab, selleth a parcel of land, which was our brother Elimelech's.
Ruth 4:1-3

Up to now Boaz had been pictured in the fields he owned. But here he was at the city gate where judicial procedures occurred. Boaz was the one in charge. Likewise, our kinsman-redeemer is the one who has all power and authority. We can trust that in every circumstance we are going through, Jesus reigns and intervenes on our behalf. Boaz had business on his mind—a strong desire to enter into covenant with Ruth. At the city gate Boaz initially spoke of the land that Naomi was selling.

The Law is All Talk and Talk is Cheap

And I thought to advertise thee, saying, Buy it before the inhabitants, and before the elders of my people. If thou wilt redeem it, redeem it: but if thou wilt not re- deem it, then tell me, that I may know: for there is none to redeem it beside thee; and I am after thee. And he said, I will redeem it.
Ruth 4:4

In this scenario the other kinsman represents the Law, and the Law says this other kinsman may re- deem the land. But his word (the Law) is not valid. Grace, represented by Boaz, is wiser than the Law. Boaz mentioned the land before he disclosed what came with the land, and that was the real treasure Boaz was after. This transaction requires the will, power and ability to redeem, and the Law cannot deliver. Only Grace can save, love and redeem. Yes, God is able. "And God is able to make all grace abound toward you; that ye, always having all sufficiency in all things, may abound to every good work" (2 Corinthians 9:8).

Raise Up the Name of the Dead? The Law Says, "No Way"!

Then said Boaz, What day thou buyest the field of the hand of Naomi, thou must buy it also of Ruth the Moabitess, the wife of the dead, to raise up the name of the dead upon his inheritance.
And the kinsman said, I cannot redeem it for myself, lest I mar mine own inheritance: redeem thou my right to thyself; for I cannot redeem it.
Ruth 4:5-6

Boaz informed the Law that he would be obligated to raise up the name of the dead upon his inheritance. Do you think the law of sin and death is interested in helping to continue to establish and build life? No! The law is weak, powerless and selfish.

The Law was looking out for his own well-being and concluded that this transaction would destroy his inheritance. After all, the law is prejudiced, exclusive, manipulative, condemning, and demanding;

but Jesus came to give life. "For what the law could not do, in that it was weak through the flesh, God sending his own Son in the likeness of sinful flesh, and for sin, condemned sin in the flesh" (Romans 8:3).

Grace is Greater By Far!

"For the law of the Spirit of life in Christ Jesus hath made me free from the law of sin and death" (Romans 8:2). When we know the truth, it makes us free. It is time for believers to believe and know the truth. We have a glorious inheritance, but we need to be acquainted with the last will and testament to see what is ours.

Read the truth from the Apostle Paul: "Now if the ministry that brought death, which was engraved in letters on stone, came with glory, so that the Israelites could not look steadily at the face of Moses because of its glory, transitory though it was, will not the ministry of the Spirit be even more glorious? If the ministry that brought condemnation was glorious, how much more glorious is the ministry that brings righteousness! For what was glorious has no glory now in comparison with the surpassing glory. And if what was transitory came with glory, how much greater is the glory of that which lasts!" (2 Corinthians 3:7-11 NIV).

What/Who is the Inheritance?

Why all the concern about the inheritance? The law of sin and death declines the proposal. Oh, but Grace! Grace gladly and with pleasure accepts! God's ways are not our ways; they are higher and better. Isaiah sheds some light: "Yet it pleased the LORD to bruise him; he hath put him to grief: when thou shalt make his soul an offering for sin, he shall see his seed, he shall prolong his days, and the pleasure of the LORD shall prosper in his hand" (Isaiah 53:10). Yes, you are the seed that prolongs His day, you are the one to establish His name in the earth, and you are His delight and pleasure that prospers in His hand!

Joshua Asks for a City

"When they had made an end of dividing the land for inheritance by their coasts, the children of Israel gave an inheritance to Joshua the son of Nun among them: According to the word of the LORD they gave him the city which he asked, even Timnath-serah in Mount Ephraim: and he built the city, and dwelt therein" (Joshua 19:49-50).

The issue at the gate concerning Boaz and the Law was inheritance, and it holds the same importance today. The book of Joshua records how the land was divided up among the sons of Israel. Joshua did not receive his inheritance until after the sons received theirs. Joshua is a "type" of the Lord Jesus Christ who takes a people into the Promised Land. Joshua asked for the city of Timnath-serah in Mount Ephraim, and he built the city and dwelt there. Let scripture interpret scripture: you are the city Jesus dwells in. "Ye are the light of the world. A city that is set on an hill cannot be hid" (Matthew 5:14).

In Hebrew *Timnath-serah* means portion of the sun, or the abundant portion, and *Ephraim* means double fruit. So the inheritance is fruitful and abundant with no limits and no boundaries. We are that city Jesus has asked for, the abundant portion, the glorious church. The inheritance of Jesus is a people for His name in union and harmony with Him.

Joshua received his inheritance after the tribes got theirs, according the word of the Lord. Jesus has yet to receive a people in His image and likeness bearing fruit.

Where is the Inheritance?
What is His Inheritance, Again?

He is our inheritance, the grandest reward of all, and we are His inheritance. The Apostle Paul will help clarify: "By having the eyes of your heart flooded with light, so that you can know and understand the hope to which He has called you, and how rich is *His glorious inheritance in the saints* (His set-apart ones), And [so that you can know and understand] what is the immeasurable and unlimited and surpassing greatness of His power in and for us who believe, as demonstrated in the working of His mighty strength, which He exerted in Christ when He raised Him from the dead and seated Him at His [own] right hand in the heavenly [places]" (Ephesians 1:18-2o AMP).

Wow, that is amazing! The glorious, abundant inheritance is found in the saints. The words of Jesus are true, "I assure you, most solemnly I tell you, Unless a grain of wheat falls into the earth and dies, it remains [just one grain; it never becomes more but lives] by itself alone. But if it dies, it produces many others and yields a rich harvest" (John 12:24 AMP). Yes, Jesus died to produce a rich harvest. He sowed his life and He will reap the abundant portion.

We, the city of Jesus, were created to live on the mountaintop in realms of spirit and life, in dimensions of love, illumination, and glory.

Inheritance by Birth

"Praised (honored, blessed) be the God and Father of our Lord Jesus Christ (the Messiah)! By His boundless mercy we have been born again to an ever-living hope through the resurrection of Jesus Christ from the dead, [Born anew] into an inheritance which is beyond the reach of change and decay [imperishable], unsullied and unfading, reserved in heaven for you" (1 Peter 1:3-4 AMP).

This glory is found in the saints as declared by Paul, "To whom God would make known what is the riches of the glory of this mystery among the Gentiles; which is Christ in you, the hope of glory" (Colossians 1:27).

This glory that is found in the saints is His inheritance. 1 Peter 1:4 says we have been "[born anew] into an inheritance which is beyond the reach of change *and* decay [imperishable], unsullied and unfading, reserved in heaven for you...." (AMP)

Strong's Exhaustive Concordance explains the Greek origin of the word *inheritance* (2817) in that scripture:

Kleronomia, meaning a possession: from *kleronomos* (in its original sense of partitioning, a sharer by lot, by implication, a possessor. From 'kleros'; probably from 'klao' by extension an acquisition (especially a patrimony, figuratively), a primary verb; to break (specially, of bread): and the base of: 'nomos'; from a primary 'nemo' (to parcel out, especially food or grazing to animals); law, specifically (of Moses [including the volume]; also of the Gospel), or figuratively (a principle).

The Greek word *klao* is used in the breaking of bread or communion. Our real inheritance is our common union or oneness with Christ! That is why it is imperative to spend time in the Word—to partake of Him.

Let us give thanks that Father God desires His city the Church to be the abundant portion. He has asked that we would be One so that the prayers of Jesus will be answered. He is the Head and we are the body that He desires to be whole, complete, full of life, living in dimensions of love and releasing glory. "Giving thanks to the Father, Who has qualified and made us fit to share the portion which is the inheritance of the saints (God's holy people) in the Light" (Colossians 1:12 AMP).

Personal Application

- In what areas of your personal life are you choosing to agree with the Word of the Lord over your life?

- What is your understanding of your inheritance in Christ Jesus?

- Expound on your inheritance using the Greek word *kleronomia*.

Chapter 7

CHANGE

Change is a necessary ingredient so we may obtain the dreams of our heart. Ruth had to change her location, her vocation, her mindset, and her friends. But her resilience and determination brought great rewards.

Think outside the box that you have been living in and learn to trust My voice and My Spirit. Without this, spirit change cannot take place, there cannot be a change in your life, a change in your circumstance, and things will not be different from the past. If you would be willing to think outside the box and allow the revelation that I have given you to be your motivation, and let the revelation then begin to create the transformation, then in your change, you will have the manifestation.

—Prophetic Word by Bishop Rick Thomas

God so wants to change and transform us and cause us to come to a place where we profoundly experience Him. God has such tremendous plans for His Church. "And to make all men see what is the fellowship of the mystery, which from the beginning of the world hath been hid in God, who created all things by Jesus Christ: To the intent that now unto the principalities and powers in heavenly places might be known by the church the manifold wisdom of God, according to the eternal purpose which he purposed in Christ Jesus our Lord" (Ephesians 3:9-11).

Paul is communicating that the plan is to put the Church on display to show off God's multifaceted wisdom. That is why it is important that we come into union with His mind, intent, heart, and purpose, which will require us to change. What changes and transforms us is His presence. God's Word says to be transformed by the renewing of your mind.

Changing is Linked to Redeeming

Now this was the manner in former time in Israel concerning redeeming and concerning changing, for to confirm all things; a man plucked off his shoe, and gave it to his neighbour: and this was a testimony in Israel.
Ruth 4:7

We have a remarkable redeemer who has purchased all things. Ownership is a central factor in both creation and redemption. If you purchase something you have a definite purpose in mind. It is no different with God. He has an intention for us to be changed.

Strong's defines *changing* in Hebrew as an "(ex-) change (-ing), recompense, restitution." God desires to exchange our life for His. What a deal!

Paul writes, "Behold, I shew you a mystery; we shall not all sleep, but we shall all be changed, in a moment, in the twinkling of an eye, at the last trump: for the trumpet shall sound, and the dead shall be raised incorruptible, and we shall be changed" (1 Corinthians 15:51-52). Mysteries are to be uncovered! The mysteries of God cannot be understood by human reasoning, only by the Spirit. The hammer of God's Word is an instrument used to mold us and shape us into His image and likeness. He is changing us from glory to glory. Our origin was in the glorious Christ as seen in the gospel of John. "And now, O Father, glorify thou me with thine own self with the glory which I had with thee before the world was" (John 17:5).

The trumpet being sounded is producing change. The "trumpet" is the sounding of the prophetic voice of God. When John the Revelator was on Patmos, he reports, "I was in the Spirit on the Lord's day, and heard behind me a great voice, as of a trumpet, saying, I am..." (Revelation 1:10-11). The trumpet is talking and God graciously keeps speaking until we understand.

Our pre-determined purpose, or destiny, is to be conformed to His image. His intention is that we shall be sons of glory. After all He is the Father of glory. "That the God of our Lord Jesus Christ, the Father of glory, may give unto you the spirit of wisdom and revelation in the knowledge of Him" (Ephesians 1:17).

Glorious Change:
A Set Time for Change

We all go through seasons which inevitably bring change. Thank God that seasons change! I get excited as this scripture is fulfilled:

> *Thou shalt arise, and have mercy upon*
> *Zion: for the time to favour her,*
> *yea, the set time, is come.*
> *For thy servants take pleasure in her*
> *stones, and favour the dust thereof. So*
> *the heathen shall fear the name of the*
> *Lord, and all the kings of the earth*
> *thy glory. When the Lord shall build up*
> *Zion, he shall appear in his glory.*
>
> Psalm 102:13-16

The Lord is edifying a people with His presence and His voice. He is building His church and the gates of hell will not prevail against it. (See Matthew 16:18.) His house will be beautiful and glorious.

Confirmation of the Property Rights

In Israel a transaction was confirmed by taking off the shoe as a symbol of the right to the property. When new owners take over, different procedures or changes transpire. We will see the wonderful blessings about to be showered on the newly redeemed one, Ruth.

The Law Says, "I Can't!"
Grace Says, "I Am Willing and Able!"

Therefore the kinsman said unto Boaz, Buy it for thee.
So he drew off his shoe.
Ruth 4:8

Here the law of sin and death has relinquished all claims or property rights. "For sin shall not have dominion over you: for ye are not under the law, but under grace" (Romans 6:14). What wonderful good news! This is a powerful business deal that points to a greater, far more superior purchase. Here Boaz is the kinsman-redeemer, but Jesus Christ is the ultimate redeemer. Paul declares, "Christ hath redeemed us from the curse of the law, being made a curse for us: for it is written, Cursed is every one that hangeth on a tree: That the blessing of Abraham might come on the Gentiles through Jesus Christ; that we might receive the promise of the Spirit through faith" (Galatians 3:13-14).

Grace Buys All

And Boaz said unto the elders, and unto all the people,
Ye are witnesses this day, that I have bought all that
was Elimelech's, and all that was Chilion's and
Mahlon's, of the hand of Naomi.
Ruth 4:9

This demonstrates that all belongs to Boaz; he bought it all. Just like Jesus paid it all, Boaz establishes full rights to all the family possessions.

Scripture says, "The earth is the LORD's, and the fulness thereof; the world, and they that dwell therein" (Psalm 24:1).

Reiteration: I Bought Ruth

Moreover Ruth the Moabitess, the wife of Mahlon, have I purchased to be my wife, to raise up the name of the dead upon his inheritance, that the name of the dead be not cut off from among his brethren, and from the gate of his place: ye are witnesses this day.
Ruth 4:10

Most women like to hear over and over that they are loved, beautiful and their beloved's number one love (after God, of course!). Boaz publicly declared his intentions and love for Ruth to all present. Likewise, Jesus redeemed His beloved bride and demonstrated His love, "But God shows and clearly proves His [own] love for us by the fact that while we were still sinners, Christ (the Messiah, the Anointed One) died for us" (Romans 5:8 AMP).

Plenty of Witnesses

*And all the people that were in the gate, and the elders,
said, We are witnesses. The LORD make the woman
that is come into thine house like Rachel and like Leah,
which two did build the house of Israel: and do thou
worthily in Ephratah, and be famous in Bethlehem:*

Ruth 4:11

Who are the witnesses and what are they wit-
nessing? They surely seem excited and all in agreement in blessing this renowned and flourishing family. These witnesses have seen and heard the testimony of Boaz and his love for Ruth and his desire to
raise up seed.

Remember, the nearer kinsman, the Law, did not
want to mar his own inheritance. But not Boaz!
There are some witnesses who seem to be just as
eager for our success, "And these all, having obtained a good report through faith, received not the
promise: God having provided some better thing for
us, that they without us should not be made perfect.
Wherefore seeing we also are compassed about with
so great a cloud of witnesses, let us lay aside every
weight, and the sin which doth so easily beset us,

and let us run with patience the race that is set before us" (Hebrews 11:39-12:1).

The promise that these witnesses are waiting for is a mature, flourishing family, a company of sons in the image of the Father. These Old Testament saints need us to finish the race. The baton has been handed off and they can't win until we win. And we are going to win because Jesus, the Victor, has won and He has made provision for us.

A Prosperous Family

Our Redeemer ushered in a new priesthood, a new order—a *change* for a specific purpose: "If therefore perfection were by the Levitical priesthood, (for under it the people received the law,) what further need was there that another priest should rise after the order of Melchisedec, and not be called after the order of Aaron? For the priesthood being *changed*, there is made of necessity a *change* also of the law.... For the law made nothing *perfect*, but the bringing in of a better hope **did**; by the which we draw nigh unto God.... By so much was Jesus made a surety of a better testament. And they truly were many priests, because they were not suffered to continue by reason of death. But this man, because he continueth ever, hath an unchangeable priesthood. Wherefore he is *able* also to save them to the uttermost that come unto God by him, seeing he ever liveth to make intercession for them" (Hebrews 7:11-12, 19, 22-25).

This new union of Boaz and Ruth was destined to be prosperous. Redeeming is linked with changing the order from law to grace, from death to life, from famine to abundance. Our identification with the new priesthood is able to establish a successful, gloriously mature family of sons in the image of Father.

A House of Increase!

And let thy house be like the house of Pharez, whom Tamar bare unto Judah, of the seed which the LORD shall give thee of this young woman.
Ruth 4:12

What else are these witnesses saying about the house of Boaz and Ruth? The name *Pharez* in Hebrew means breaking, breaking forth, bursting forth, broken walls, and increase. In Micah, Jesus is called the Breaker: "The Breaker [the Messiah] will go up before them. They will break through, pass in through the gate and go out through it, and their King will pass on before them, the Lord at their head" (Micah 2:13 AMP).

As the nature of Christ is birthed and manifested within us, the Breaker will bring breakthroughs. Walls of limitation and lack are broken as we live out of the new order of life. The presence of the Breaker brings change and in your change is the manifestation!

Personal Application

- What changes or growth do you see occurring in your walk with God?

- What do you understand about the great cloud of witnesses? What significance is it that "they, without us, should not be made perfect"?

- In your own life how has "change" brought you increase?

- Remembering that "God is able," what breakthroughs are you believing for?

Chapter 8

FATHER HAS A PURPOSE: AN ANOINTED, PERFECTED FAMILY

I have the best Dad in the world. He loves my Mom, he loves me and my younger sister, and there is nothing he would not do for us. As wonderful as my earthly dad is, he can't compare to our heavenly Father. Abba Daddy does not just have love—He is love. It is Father's good pleasure to give us the kingdom. Father provides for every need, and that is why He instituted the covenant of marriage.

Union Produces Fruit

So Boaz took Ruth, and she was his wife: and when he went in unto her, the LORD gave her conception, and she bare a son.
Ruth 4:13

The season of love is here. I believe that God speaks through various means. When we last celebrated Groundhog Day and the rodent did not see his shadow, it supposedly signified an early end to winter. I shouted, "Hallelujah," because Solomon had said the same thing years ago, "For, lo, the winter is past; the rain is over and gone; the flowers appear on the earth; the time of the singing (of birds) is come, and the voice of the turtle-dove is heard in our land" (Song of Songs 2:11-12 ASV).

Do you hear it? Love is in the air. John the revelator heard the sound: "Let us rejoice and be exceeding glad, and let us give the glory unto him: for the marriage of the Lamb is come, and his wife hath made herself ready. And it was given unto her that she should array herself in fine linen, bright (and) pure: for the fine linen is the righteous acts of the saints" (Revelation 19:7-8 ASV).

Our time of union with our heavenly Boaz is now. He is calling or inviting us to a deeper place of intimacy and out of that relationship of adoration and love He desires fruit. What a time of celebration when the bundle of joy, the son arrived for Boaz, Ruth and the community!

Prophetic Destiny Produces

The birth of the most significant seed, Jesus, was dependent on Ruth ending up in the right field. We are going to look at three additional women in scripture who bore significant seed: The Church, Elizabeth and Mary. The Father wants His Church to bear fruit, which is the nature of Christ. This is Paul's prayer, "My little children, of whom I travail in birth again until Christ be formed in you" (Galatians 4:19). The Living Bible says it this way, "Oh, my children, how you are hurting me! I am once again suffering for you the pains of a mother waiting for her child to be born-longing for the time when you will finally be filled with Christ" (Galatians 4:19).

In scripture, *woman* usually represents the soul realm or the Church. This was David speaking, "My soul shall make her boast in the LORD: the humble shall hear thereof, and be glad" (Psalm 34:2). This woman, representing the Church, was clothed with the sun: "And there appeared a great wonder in heaven; a woman clothed with the sun, and the moon under her feet, and upon her head a crown of twelve stars: And she being with child cried, travailing in birth, and pained to be delivered...and the dragon stood before the woman which was ready to be delivered, for to devour her child as soon as it was born. And she brought forth a man child, who was to rule all nations with a rod of iron: and her child was caught up unto God, and to his throne" (Revelation 12:1-2, 4b-5).

Let scripture interpret scripture, "For the LORD God is a sun and shield..." (Psalm 84:11). This woman has such a relationship with God the Son, He is her garment and covering.

And she had a crown of twelve stars on her head or mind. Stars point us to the celestial region and speak of glory. "There is one glory of the sun, and another glory of the moon, and another glory of the stars: for one star differeth from another star in glory" (1 Corinthians 15:41). The woman in the book of Revelation had glory on her mind, and the number twelve speaks of divine government. She is submitted to the Lordship of Jesus Christ.

She is travailing to bring forth, which is exactly where we are. The soul, or woman, is in a place to bring forth the desire of all nations, the manifestation of the glory of God. "And I will shake all nations, and the desire of all nations shall come: and I will fill this house with glory, saith the LORD of hosts. The silver is mine, and the gold is mine, saith the LORD of hosts. The glory of this latter house shall be greater than of the former, saith the LORD of hosts: and in this place will I give peace, saith the LORD of hosts" (Haggai 2:7-9).

This is a picture of the kingdom of God on earth as it is in heaven. We are pregnant with purpose, a divine destiny, and we are brought into the kingdom for such a time as this. The manchild is coming forth because nothing can stop the seed. The seed is the Word, Jesus Christ, who lives within us. "Being born again, not of corruptible seed, but of incorruptible, by the word of God, which liveth and abideth for ever" (1 Peter 1:23).

Extraordinary Offspring

In the gospel of Luke we have the account of Mary and Elizabeth, both of whom birthed extraordinary offspring: the prophet of the Highest and the Son of the Highest. (See Luke 1:76.)

"And the angel said unto her, Fear not, Mary: for thou hast found favour with God. And, behold, thou shalt conceive in thy womb, and bring forth a son, and shalt call his name JESUS. He shall be great, and shall be called the Son of the Highest: and the Lord God shall give unto him the throne of his father David: And he shall reign over the house of Jacob for ever; and of his kingdom there shall be no end. Then said Mary unto the angel, How shall this be, seeing I know not a man? And the angel answered and

said unto her, The Holy Ghost shall come upon thee, and the power of the Highest shall overshadow thee: therefore also that holy thing which shall be born of thee shall be called the Son of God. And, behold, thy cousin Elisabeth, she hath also conceived a son in her old age: and this is the sixth month with her, who was called barren. For with God nothing shall be impossible. And Mary said, Behold the handmaid of the Lord; be it unto me according to thy word. And the angel departed from her. And Mary arose in those days, and went into the hill country with haste, into a city of Juda; And entered into the house of Zacharias, and saluted Elisabeth. And it came to pass, that, when Elisabeth heard the salutation of Mary, the babe leaped in her womb; and Elisabeth was filled with the Holy Ghost: And she spake out with a loud voice, and said, Blessed art thou among women, and blessed is the fruit of thy womb. And whence is this to me, that the mother of my Lord should come to me? For, lo, as soon as the voice of thy salutation sounded in mine ears, the babe leaped in my womb for joy. And blessed is she that believed: for there shall be a performance of those things which were told her from the Lord. And Mary said, My soul doth magnify the Lord, And my spirit hath rejoiced in God my Saviour. For he hath regarded the low estate of his handmaiden: for, behold, from henceforth all generations shall call me blessed. For he that is mighty hath done to me great things; and holy is his name... And Mary abode with her about three months, and returned to her own house."

Luke 1:30-49, 56

Holy Spirit Infilling

Just as the Holy Ghost overshadowed Mary, the Holy Spirit desires to permeate you. We would do well to respond as she did saying, "Be it unto me according to your word!" Mary got into agreement with the Word, aligned with the Word, and believed. Then she arose and went in an attitude of praise all the way to see Elizabeth.

We need to get to a higher place in the Spirit to have God's perspective and to participate in His plan. Mary's voice caused Elizabeth's baby to leap. Powerful! What effect is our sound creating? These two women conceived and birthed prophetic, divine destiny. We can learn a few principles from them for our own journey of birthing our divine destiny:

- Be connected and joined with those who carry a similar purpose. Like Mary, you are carrying a prophetic, redeeming, delivering destiny. You are a type of Mary who is pregnant with purpose.

- Be attached to the more sure word of prophecy-The Word. The prophetic yet unborn within Elizabeth leaps for joy at Mary's salutation (voice, sound). John's purpose was to prepare the way of Jesus. John did not move until Jesus stepped into the room.

- Recognize that when the Holy Ghost joins us to our Elizabeth, we, like Elizabeth and Mary, can prophesy with boldness. They cooperate with the synergy of the Holy Spirit and bless each other's unique assignment.

- God supernaturally connects you to those who celebrate you, your purpose and destiny. They are committed and bring encouragement and blessings in the process.

- Be confident and expect and declare that there shall be a performance. Release your faith! Believe and receive!

Blessings Produce Fame

And the women said unto Naomi, Blessed be the LORD, which hath not left thee this day without a kinsman, that his name may be famous in Israel.
Ruth 4:14

This sure was a right-on word. God is no respecter of persons. "Verily, verily, I say unto you,

He that believeth on me, the works that I do shall he do also; and greater works than these shall he do; because I go unto my Father" (John 14:12). The time of supernatural astonishing miracles is now!

Glorious Restoration

And he shall be unto thee a restorer of thy life, and a nourisher of thine old age: for thy daughter in law, which loveth thee, which is better to thee than seven sons, hath born him.
Ruth 4:15

God is a restorer in supernatural proportions. His purposes for Naomi, Ruth and the Church at large are splendid. The word *restore* in Hebrew means to return, answer, repair, to bring back to mind, to reverse, deliver, recover, to be restored, to be brought back. It is Obed, the son of Boaz and Ruth, who is being named the kinsman. He is credited with being a restorer and rightly so. Obed creates a restoration process for Naomi because with his birth she has new purpose. This child had a supernatural ability to renew and replenish supply. Obed's name means "worshiping servant who dresses and tills the land."

In order for there to be restoration there needs to be one who will worship, honor the Lord, and till the land. A plowman is needed to work the ground for increase. Praise, or Judah, is seen in this capacity. "… Judah shall plow, and Jacob shall break his clods. Sow to yourselves in righteousness, reap in mercy; break up your fallow ground: for it is time to seek the LORD, till he come and rain righteousness upon you" (Hosea 10:11b-12). This sounds like Obed, the worshiping servant who tills and plows until there is rain of righteousness. The rain of righteousness is one-third of the kingdom of God: "For the Kingdom of God is not meat and drink; but righteousness [1/3], and peace [1/3], and joy in the Holy Ghost [1/3]" (Romans 14:17).

God wants all of heaven's reality to invade earth. As Obed worships, he is in the presence of God and the Word tells us what is in His presence: "Thou wilt shew me the path of life: in thy presence is fulness of joy; at thy right hand there are pleasures for evermore" (Psalm 16:11). Joy is one of the other parts of the Kingdom of God.

Wow! Obed is a life changer! He is a restorer of life and the Word says, "Peacemakers who sow in peace raise a harvest of righteousness" (James 3:18 NIV). Obed is a kingdom man, who seems to be demonstrating peace, another third of the Kingdom of God.

These are words from the offspring of Obed, King David, "Let them shout for joy, and be glad, that favour my righteous cause: yea, let them say continually, Let the LORD be magnified, which hath pleasure in the prosperity of his servant" (Psalm 35:27). And the progeny of King David, Jesus, said, "Fear not, little flock; for it is your Father's good pleasure to give you the kingdom" (Luke 12:32). And, as Bishop Thomas would say, "Let me bring Him pleasure."

God has a glorious plan of restoration and supernatural living. Just as Obed was a restorer, there are many more like him. "And they that shall be of thee shall build the old waste places: thou shalt raise up the foundations of many generations; and thou shalt be called, the repairer of the breach, the restorer of paths to dwell in" (Isaiah 58:12).

Our purpose is to direct people back to the Father, the source. Jesus is the way, the truth and the life. God desires a family of sons in His image and likeness who are fruitful and abundantly supplied. This "Obed company" reminds me of a portion of a prophesy given in 2011 by Bishop Rick Thomas:

My Holy Spirit will be felt; My Word will be kept; and My blessings released! You shall know My presence. You will experience My promises and you will operate in My favor and MY prosperity!

Obed's mother, Ruth, was a productive woman. She knew and mastered the law of sowing and reaping. We saw how she sowed into Naomi, sowed into the city and how she reaped an incredible harvest—part of which is Boaz and Obed. She has such a reputation that even the neighbors see the anointing of miraculous increase and sing her praise.

Glorious Anointing of Prosperity

The neighbors say she is kinder and better than seven sons. This deserves more attention, for a woman to be better than seven sons is nothing short of supernatural. The Hebrew word for better is *towb* which means beautiful, bountiful, cheerful, favour, fine, glad, good, graciously, joyful, kindly, kindness, liketh (best), loving, merry, most pleasant, pleasure, precious, prosperity, ready, sweet, wealth, (be) well favoured. She is some woman! And that is not all.

Seven sons are proverbial for the perfect family. Paul explains the complete perfect family, "Till we all come in the unity of the faith, and of the knowledge of the Son of God, unto a perfect man, unto the measure of the stature of the fulness of Christ" (Ephesians 4:13).

Recently I was ministering at a church and stayed with a family that is a living demonstration of a beautiful, functioning, unified family. The husband is in love with his wife, she respects and honors him, and the children all display a healthy, serving attitude towards each other—truly lovely.

The Father will have His desire. Jesus prayed that we all would be one. "And the glory which thou gavest me I have given them; that they may be one, even as we are one: I in them, and thou in me, that they may be made perfect in one; and that the world may know that thou hast sent me, and hast loved them, as thou hast loved me" (John 17:22-23). The glory is given so we will experience oneness with the Lord. The mind of Christ must be in operation as well as the fullness of the Spirit (the seven-fold Spirit of sonship) which rested on Jesus and is now upon us, His body by our virtue of being one with Him.

Then a shoot will spring from the stem of Jesse, And a branch from his roots will bear fruit. And the Spirit of the LORD will rest on Him, The spirit of wisdom and understanding, The spirit of counsel and strength,

The spirit of knowledge and the fear of the LORD. And He will delight in the fear of the LORD, And He will not judge by what His eyes see, Nor make a decision by what His ears hear; But with

righteousness He will judge the poor,
And decide with fairness for the afflicted
of the earth; And He will strike the
earth with the rod of His mouth,
And with the breath of His lips
He will slay the wicked.
Isaiah 11:1-4 NASB

This is the Spirit that is like a glory cloud resting upon the sons of God. The anointing that rested upon the head is the same anointing that flows in His body. The seven Spirits of God which is the Holy Ghost full of power will be operating in the end-time Church. We see that the source of this mighty outworking of power is the Lamb. "And I saw in the midst of the throne and of the four living creatures, and in the midst of the elders, a Lamb standing, as though it had been slain, having seven horns, and seven eyes, which are the seven Spirits of God, sent forth into all the earth" (Revelation 5:6 ASV).

Ruth, the wife of Boaz, is described as better than seven sons, and the bride of Jesus will be all that and more. Jesus said, "I am the vine, ye are the branches: He that abideth in me, and I in him, the same bringeth forth much fruit: for without me ye can do nothing" (John 15:5). And Isaiah prophesied about the branch. "In that day shall the branch of the LORD be beautiful and glorious, and the fruit of the earth shall be excellent and comely..." (Isaiah 4:2).

We are royalty; it is time to act like it. "But ye are a chosen generation, a royal priesthood, an holy nation, a peculiar people; that ye should shew forth the praises of him who hath called you out of darkness into his marvellous light" (1 Peter 2:9).

The Neighbors Name the Revival!

> And Naomi took the child, and laid it in her bosom, and became nurse unto it. And the women her neighbours gave it a name, saying, There is a son born to Naomi; and they called his name Obed: he is the father of Jesse, the father of David.
> Ruth 4:16-17

Talk about changing a city for God! And remember, this was in the Old Testament. The season that is upon the Church of Jesus Christ—if you can put it into words—is more closely aligned to the expression of Habakkuk, which Paul picked up on, "... for I work a work in your days, a work which ye shall in no wise believe, though a man declare it unto you" (Acts 13:41).

Father's redemptive plan has not left anyone out. Naomi and Ruth were unlikely candidates and the neighbors even got involved. It is unusual that the neighbors named the child, but the supernatural workings of a providential God were so obvious they felt entitled to do so.

The Glorious New Generation

Now these are the generations of Pharez: Pharez begat Hezron, And Hezron begat Ram, and Ram begat Amminadab, And Amminadab begat Nahshon, and Nahshon begat Salmon, And Salmon begat Boaz, and Boaz begat Obed, And Obed begat Jesse, and Jesse begat David.
Ruth 4:18 - 22

We are nearing the end of our journey in the book of Ruth. We close with the listing of the generations in the lineage of King Jesus and by extension *you*. A name denotes nature and reveals a purpose that is being birthed. All those in the lineage of Messiah have significant meaning and they all have characteristics of people with covenant hearts.

We will look at the Hebrew meaning of each name to trace an unfolding of incredible importance and the significant miraculous intention of our Father:

- Pharez: breaker or breaking forth. Can you see where you have come out of limitations? Fears that once paralyzed you have vanished. Insecurities that distracted have been replaced by the presence of God. Your Christ nature has broken through!

- Hezron: surrounded by a wall, to sound a trumpet. Once you have overcome a challenge you are fortified and have something to shout about.

- Ram: high, exalted, to be raised. As you sound your trumpet the flow of His presence is increasing.

- Amminadab: my kinsman is noble, my people are willing, a liberal giver. As God is exalted (Ram) He exalts His family. An increase of His presence increases generosity in our lives; it is His nature.

- Nashon: divine experience. God leads from glory to glory, from faith to faith.

- Salmon: garment, mantle. Our Father desires that we are clothed and saturated with His glorious presence.

- Boaz: fleetness or strength, name of the left pillar in Solomon's temple. "A wise man is strong; yea, a man of knowledge increaseth strength" (Proverbs 24:5).

- Obed: worshipping servant.

- Jesse: I possess, existence, substance. Faith has to be part of the equation. "Now faith is the substance of things hoped for, the evidence of things not seen" (Hebrews 11:1).

- David: beloved. You are loved to love so that you can love others.

Our Father knew from generation to generation the exact process and the connections that needed to occur for divine alignment to birth His purpose on the earth. He knew the end from the beginning. The process brought the purpose to manifestation. God's purpose on the earth is to have a family of sons in His image and likeness to be His glory and praise.

The Generation of Jesus Christ

Matthew, the disciple of Jesus, wrote to the Jewish converts and begins his Gospel with these words, "The book of the generation of Jesus Christ, the son of David, the son of Abraham" (Matthew 1:1). A generation is something being born and coming forth in relation to nature. "And Jacob begat Joseph the husband of Mary, of whom was born Jesus, who is called Christ. So all the generations from Abraham to David are fourteen generations; and from David until the carrying away into Babylon are fourteen generations; and from the carrying away into Babylon unto Christ are fourteen generations" (Matthew 1:16-17).

Jechonias was the twenty-eighth generation and if you count from verse 12 through the next fourteen generations, you will find that Jesus is the forty-first and Christ is the forty-second generation. We are the forty-second generation: the number six for man times seven for perfection is the generation of Jesus Christ.

The forty-second generation is the Father's perfected family of compassionate servers and passionate worshippers who are manifesting Christ. "When Christ, Who is our life, appears, then you also will appear with Him in [the splendor of His] glory" (Colossians 3:4 AMP).

Worship is a lifestyle of giving God the worth He deserves. What divine providence! Only God could execute such a plan. "He raiseth up the poor out of the dust, and lifteth up the beggar from the dunghill, to set them among princes, and to make them inherit the throne of glory: for the pillars of the earth are the LORD's, and he hath set the world upon them" (1 Samuel 2:8).

"And He raised us up together with Him and made us sit down together [giving us joint seating with Him] in the heavenly sphere [by virtue of our being] in Christ Jesus (the Messiah, the Anointed One)" (Ephesians 2:6 AMP).

The 42nd Generation's Common Mission

Matthew ends his book with our kingdom mandate or commission: GO! "And when they saw him, they worshipped him: but some doubted. And Jesus came and spake unto them, saying, All power is given unto me in heaven and in earth. Go ye therefore, and teach all nations, baptizing them in the name of the Father, and of the Son, and of the Holy Ghost: Teaching them to observe all things whatsoever I have commanded you: and, lo, I am with you alway, even unto the end of the world. Amen" (Matthew 28:17-20).

Just as Ruth played a major role in human history, God has chosen and destined *you* for this supernatural time, to be part of His glorious redemptive plan on the earth. Jesus has given the marching orders to His disciples. His instructions are still in force and the accomplishing will be by His Spirit.

There is a freshly compounded anointing fused with empowerment from the Father to the Generation of Jesus to be His glorious expression of the Bride of Christ who is our true identity.

Personal Application

- What desire has been placed in your heart by the Holy Spirit?

- What causes your baby to leap, meaning what stirs you to get excited about your reason for existence, your purpose?

- Like Mary (Luke 1:49) and Ruth, what great things has God done for you?

- What does it mean to you that Ruth is seen by the neighbors as being better than seven sons?

- What are you believing for?

- What is your understanding of the 42nd Generation?

Chapter 9

DREAMS FULFILLED

I promised at the beginning of this book to tell you how my journey has progressed. Like Ruth, God provided me with a providential journey.

One day an invitation came for me to minister in Hawaii and enjoy some rest and relaxation. I immediately wondered when I could go because I was still recovering from the effects of the accident." But, to my surprise, my doctor cleared me to travel. And, oh, what a trip! My spirit began to revive immediately. The physical beauty of the islands was breath-taking even from the air!

I arrived at the Hilo airport where I was met by a wonderful couple and a tall, handsome minister and prophet, Ken Purvis. The connection between Ken and me was immediate. He took me to lunch to eat Thai food, a favorite for both of us. That night we went to see a movie, "The Help," which was filmed in his hometown of Greenwood, Mississippi. I had a great feeling of peace —it felt like paradise.

After the first day I called Mom to tell her I had had the best day of my life. That first day was quickly outdone by the second! Ken and I took a six-hour hike where we gazed upon one beautiful sight after another. We stopped along the way for lunch. He prayed and my spirit was overwhelmed as though a tidal wave had overtaken me. It was on that day he said, "I may be your covenant promise."

Later we went to a cozy French restaurant for a delicious dinner. There we discovered more and more that our desires were similar in regard to our purpose and desire for the Kingdom. On the third day Ken asked me for an official date at the Volcano

Cave on our way to a jazz concert. That was the day he said to me, "I've been waiting for you all my life."

We met in the month of December, so we went to see the Nutcracker Suite, and just enjoyed the moments with each other. I had an opportunity to speak with Ken's mother by phone, and I told her what a great son she had. Was it really only five days that we had known each other? Every day brought one delight after another.

After a walk in a beautiful tropical garden in Hilo, we went swimming. At that moment a prophetic word I had received awakened in me, "It will overtake you like a tidal wave." It had been twenty years since I received that word. Now it was actually happening, and God knew all along the place, the time and the person.

On the sixth night I had a dream, and in the dream a woman said to me, "He is a good man; you should relate to him." This was the day Ken bought me a pair of walking shoes, telling me, "We have a compatible walk. Walk with me. You are everything I have asked for."

It was then I remembered my prayer and song for my husband. You see, I had prayed for my husband-to-be during those twenty-plus years, fasting for him and even singing to him in the spirit. I gave him the name, "Chenaniah" (1 Chronicles 15:22, 27), and I wrote two songs about a psalmist with whom I would share my desire to worship.

The eighth day was another unique day. Ken found two silver quarters the same morning I was reading Psalm 111. Specifically verse 9 stood out which reads, *"He sent redemption unto his people: He hath commanded his covenant for ever: holy and reverend is his name."* Silver speaks of redemption, God's original intention. It was this day Ken said, "I am going to ask you something bold. Will you marry me?" I asked him, "When or will you be coming to Florida?"

I called my dad. He and Mother already had a sense of something supernatural taking place. Ken and I went on another hiking adventure, watching surfers catching waves, waiting for just the right one. I looked up toward the clouds and saw the shape of a cup, and sensed the Father was saying, "Receive My blessings."

I wrote a note to Ken saying, "Thank you for being a facilitator of making my dreams a reality." It had been an overwhelmingly wonderful ten days. Every day was a beautiful unfolding, an awakening to love — the love of the Father and a love I had desired for decades. A close friend of Ken's came by to make us the most delicious French dinner, and that night I dreamed I was getting married.

On my fourteenth day in Hawaii, Ken anointed my feet for the walk. The following day I was returning to Florida. The goodbyes were hard but tempered by the fact that I would see him in Florida for Christmas.

Sitting on the plane, I had time for reflection. I said, "Lord, You outdid Yourself!" Miracles do happen. Stories do have happy endings. There is hope for dreams becoming a reality when God is in it.

In January I went on a twenty-one day liquid fast in preparation for our wedding, seeking answers from the Father: "Father, when is our wedding date?" A few days later I called forth my ring in the spirit.

In the beginning of February Ken and I went to Mississippi so I could meet his mother, and from there to Texas where he had been asked to minister at a conference. I had asked God for a promise and was led to Proverbs 10:24b, *"but the desire of the righteous shall be granted."*

After the conference we had breakfast with Ken's Bishop. It happened to be Valentine's Day— what a divine set-up! Together we discussed church matters, but then the talk grew more personal. At the conference the Bishop declared to the congregation the need to get into agreement with what God desires for your life, and in seven days it will manifest. The Bishop asked Ken what he had asked for. It was the date for our wedding. My request was for a ring. So I blurted out, "Let's set a date *now!*" So the Bishop wrote a date, I wrote a date, and Ken... got out his calendar. The Bishop turned to him and said, "Put your calendar away and ask the Holy Spirit." Well, both the Bishop and I had written the same date, which was about a month away.

When we returned to Florida, it was the seventh day since I had come into agreement with God for my ring. At a breakfast sponsored by the Christian International Businessmen, I told a dear friend what had been transpiring in my life. She impressed on us that it was important that we come to her house after the meeting. When we arrived, my friend pulled out a box with rings for both of us. My prayer was answered in epic proportions!

Ken formally proposed to me in front of my mother and father. He gave my mother a rose. Then, on his knees, he presented one to me with the ring on the stem. All of us were overcome with emotion and felt the blessing of the presence of God.

Supernatural Dream Moment

My dream moment arrived on a day of spiritual significance for me. The stage was set and the wedding arrangements had come together in a few short weeks with help from all directions. It was March 17, 2012. March is the third month of the year and the number three means complete or divine perfection. The seventeenth day of the month was the day Noah's ark landed on Mount Ararat, signifying the end of destruction.

For me it was a day of reversal and restoration. Now I could

enter into a brand new world
through the experience of a
God-ordained
covenant relationship.

Seventeen combines the number 7, representing spiritual perfection, and the number 10 representing ordinal perfection. Together they speak of spiritual order. What bliss when marriage is entered into with the Father's blessing—naturally and spiritually!

With my mother playing the piano, Ken accompanied her with the trumpet, prophetically calling "Sally," his bride, to a union operating in kingdom principles. The sanctuary was filled with the presence of God as Bishop Rick Thomas officiated an awesome ceremony. One of his words to us was, "Destiny must come and kiss the purpose that is in their lives now."

A few days later Mr. and Mrs. Robert Kendall Purvis embarked on a glorious honeymoon cruise. God's favor continued to smile on us. Out of 4,500 passengers, we were invited to sit at the Captain's table for a magnificent dinner.

Ministry Together

God is only moved by His plans and purpose. As a couple we embraced the next step in our calling and destiny, allowing the Holy Spirit to move us into another "first." As our Father would have it, our ministry, "The Glorious Restoration," was launched May 27th 2012, in Fort Lauderdale on the Day of Pentecost.

> ## As part of this ancient observance Pentecost is the day when the Book of Ruth is read.

For us it was an awesome holy convocation as we ministered on how Pentecost impacts us today and the importance of coming into agreement with Heaven. It was a personal new beginning for us and for many who attended. We reconnected to the glorious infilling of the power of the Holy Spirit as we celebrated the ordained appointment of the Feast of Shavuot. "To everything there is a season, and a time to every purpose under the heaven" (Ecclesiastes 3:1 KJV).

The experience of Pentecost expressed in Acts 2 birthed the New Testament Church through the outpouring of "the Promise of the Father." The present observance would be our appointed season further revealing the Father's predetermined purpose and destiny. For those faithful disciples of Jesus everything changed-in a *kairos* (God-appointed) moment —a new administration was inaugurated. For us also it was another new beginning, a restoration of ministry.

A prophetic irony occurred when our scheduled meeting room was flooded by a torrential outpouring of rain and we had to be moved into an adjoining room. It was not until the end of the service that one of the attendees pointed out a life-sized statue that looked like Ruth holding two sheaves, standing directly behind us. We truly saw God's hand of providence and care.

When seen against the mirror of the true love that Ken and I share, I saw the shallowness of past relationships, much as Ruth must have felt when she experienced the worship of the One True God in contrast to the idol worship of the Moabites. I could say, in truth, my past is over and the best is yet to come!

RESOURCE

Biblesoft's New Exhaustive Strong's Numbers and Concordance with Expanded Greek-Hebrew Dictionary. Copyright © 1994, 2003 Biblesoft, Inc. and International Bible Translators, Inc.

THE AUTHOR

Sally Smith Purvis has found a place of intimacy with the Father, and is an anointed revelational preacher with a prophetic mantle. She has ministered for over 20 years nationally and internationally in conferences, Bible schools and local churches. Her passion is to know Him and the power of His resurrection and to release His life, joy and truth to set people free.